Getting to Know Death

NOVELS

Old Lovegood Girls (2020)

Grief Cottage (2017)

Flora (2013)

Unfinished Desires (2009)

Queen of the Underworld (2006)

Evenings at Five (2003)

Evensong (2009)

The Good Husband (1994)

Father Melancholy's Daughter (1991)

A Southern Family (1987)

The Finishing School (1984)

A Mother and Two Daughters (1982)

Violet Clay (1978)

The Odd Woman (1974)

Glass People (1972)

The Perfectionists (1970)

STORY COLLECTIONS

Mr. Bedford and the Muses (1983)

Dream Children (1976)

NONFICTION

Publishing: A Writer's Memoir (2015)

The Making of a Writer: Journals, vols. 1 and 2 (2006, 2011),

edited by Rob Neufeld

Heart: A Personal Journry through Its Myths and Meanings

(2001)

Getting to Know Death

A Meditation

Gail Godwin

BLOOMSBURY PUBLISHING
NEW YORK · LONDON · OXFORD · NEW DELHI · SYDNEY

BLOOMSBURY PUBLISHING
Bloomsbury Publishing Inc.
1385 Broadway, New York, NY 10018, USA

BLOOMSBURY, BLOOMSBURY PUBLISHING, and the Diana logo
are trademarks of Bloomsbury Publishing Plc

First published in the United States in 2024

ISBN: HB: 978-1-63973-444-3; EBOOK: 978-1-63973-445-0

LIBRARY OF CONGRESS CATALOGING-IN-PUBLICATION DATA IS AVAILABLE

2 4 6 8 10 9 7 5 3 1

Typeset by Westchester Publishing Services
Printed and bound in the U.S.A.

To find out more about our authors and books visit www.bloomsbury.com
and sign up for our newsletters.

Bloomsbury books may be purchased for business or promotional use. For
information on bulk purchases please contact Macmillan Corporate and
Premium Sales Department at specialmarkets@macmillan.com.

Live dyingly

—CHRISTOPHER HITCHENS, IN HIS LAST DAYS

GG to Therapist: Who is Steph?

Therapist: Steph who?

GG: When I said the only place where I felt safe these days was inside my novel, you said, "What if you stepped outside that place and started getting to know Steph?"

T: No, I said "death." Getting to know death.

Getting to Know Death

I

Robert liked to quote Ingmar Bergman: "An artist should always have one work between himself and death." He had finished a short work, "The Lake," intended to be a section of a longer work, on the spring evening before he was carried out from our house at dawn by the Woodstock Rescue Squad. The organist played the penciled draft of "The Lake" at his funeral.

June 6, 2022. Is my present novel, half-done, destined to be the work between me and death? Yesterday I thought I had completed Part One, but this morning I realized A. needed to address how she felt about her employer's unusual "family pact." And wonder how she will look back on this time in future years.

So necessary! But I only saw such a necessity after I had written it down.

June 6, afternoon

The little dogwood tree, planted last week, is languishing in the hot sun. First it was four feet high, then the deer ate off the crown and all the white blossoms. Midafternoon on a Monday. Too early for Deadline: White House, *with Nicolle Wallace.*

You decide to water the little tree. You plan what is to be done. Take your walking cane for extrabalance security when you reach the ground cover and the rocks between the gravel and the faucet for the house. Then out the door, down the stone steps, turn right on the gravel, walk with cane thirty to forty feet to the spot at the corner of the house where the faucet hides between the vinca and the rocks.

Done. Then cross over carefully, still with cane, and bend down to grasp the faucet. Twist to the right.

Now for the retreat, stepping cautiously backward through the thicket of vinca, avoiding the rocks.

You muster resolve. Gravel lies in front of you. Step into it with cane, and turn right toward the little dogwood tree.

A wavering pause. A doubt, a loss of nerve. A wobble through space, and you're falling forward.

WHAP.

You are down. Flat on your face in the gravel.

It has happened.

Your head and neck are twisted to the left.

Blood dripping onto the gravel.

Your head and shoulders are in the hot sun.

If you could crawl backward into the vinca shade you might lie down and take a little nap.

No.

Can you stand up? Face another wobble in space? Risk another WHAP?

You calculate the distance you must cross to reach those steps you just descended. Thirty feet? From here it looks like more.

How to move your body across that space without standing up?

First, sit up.

Best move after sitting up: butt-walk, straight ahead, one cheek then the other. Right left, right left.

You feel the gravel cutting through your faithful tan corduroy pants.

Keep butt-walking and eventually this will be over.

Cheek by cheek in the tan corduroy pants.

Will I make it to those steps?

I really don't know.

Do you WANT to make it?

I'm not sure.

Yes or no?

I feel more curiosity than I feel resolve.

That will have to suffice. Inch forward, one cheek then the other. Be glad it's corduroy, not thin cotton.

What is this about your neck. You keep wanting to stretch it. You move it from side to side.

*Keep going! Don't stop now. Keep pulling your cane along
with you.*

One cheek, then the other, right, left, ouch, ouch.

At last. Crawl up the steps.

*Lie down and rest on the stone porch. Then plan for the final
heave-ho. Iron railings.*

*Drag yourself across with your left hand, pulling your cane as
you go. One, two, three, four. Four iron railings.*

*Here's another challenge: you need to grip the fourth railing
and raise yourself to a kneeling position in order to open the door.*

Wriggle over the threshold. Bring the cane.

Crawl into the entrance room.

See if you can stand up.

*No, steady against the wall first. Then slowly rise, hand flat
against the wall. Follow along wall to the kitchen.*

Pull over the chair next to the telephone.

Punch in 911.

*You know the drill from here. You did it before, for Robert,
twenty-one years ago.*

"I want you to send the Woodstock Rescue Squad."

The fireman arrives first.

"Hello? Hello?"

"I'm here in the kitchen."

"Oh, there you are."

He rounds the corner. Somewhere in the past, I would have described him as a nice older man.

"What did you do?"

"I fell on my face out there in the gravel and couldn't stand up. So I butt-walked to the house and crawled up the steps."

"Wow." He stands above me, looking me over. "There's blood on your face, but I'm going to wait for the EMT to get here. What happened out there?"

"I was on my way to water a new dogwood tree, and I lost nerve and fell."

"Why do you keep stretching your neck like that?"

"Because it feels a little funny."

"Well, don't move it any more till the EMT gets here. Last year we pulled a woman out of a car and she was paralyzed from the neck down. The EMT will have a temporary brace to stabilize it. You don't want that neck to be flopping around in the ambulance. I think I hear them."

A youngish man and a youngish woman in uniform enter, and immediately after, a third, in street clothes. I recognize him! He was here with the team that carried Robert out twenty-one years ago. In street clothes then, too.

The temporary neck brace has been fitted, the blood has been patted rather than washed from the face with a damp kitchen towel. They are all standing around me. Do I live alone? What do I need to take with me, and what do I need for someone to do here? Twenty-one years ago, they scooped Robert's two shelves of medications into a gallon-sized ziplock bag, but the fireman is delighted when I tell him to pull a notecard from my purse. It has all my meds (ten of them) listed. "I always carry a couple."

The cat descends the staircase.

"What about her?"

"It's a him. Would you mind calling this one person, she can take care of it all."

After the fireman punches in the numbers, he reassures whoever has answered the phone, "First I want to tell you everything's all right."

My purse. A wrap in case it gets cold. I transfer myself from the chair to the stretcher and lie down. Robert couldn't lie down because of his heart. He had to be carried to the ambulance like a sitting pharaoh. They are in their places. The EMTs in back, the fireman at the right front, and, at the left front, the person who was here for the carry-out twenty-one years ago. How can he look exactly the same? Slightly built, solemn, even the clothes seem the same. "I remember you," I tell him. He looks at me but doesn't speak. I've never heard him speak. He must be in his forties or fifties by now, but he looks exactly the same.

Up we go. I feel sad remembering how hard it was for four people to carry Robert out the door.

I am lifted with a final heave into the rear doors of the ambulance. "This is our new ambulance," the woman tells me. The fireman heads for his truck and the silent man for his car. An uncanny link between this day and that.

"Can you think of anything I can do for you when I come back to get my car?" asks the woman.

"Yes. You see that far corner of the house? There's a faucet connected to a hose. I was going to water that little dogwood tree. Would you water it and then turn off the faucet?"

Riding backward down the long, familiar driveway. My head in its brace is elevated and I can look out the window. It's the beginning of June, the month of my eighty-fifth birthday. I'm surrounded by the rich bright green of new leaves. The leaves were still tiny red furls in mid-April of 2001.

"I'm the neurosurgeon. You broke your neck. You have too many issues for surgery. You will wear a hard collar for six months. The fracture will mend or it won't. Meanwhile tissue will grow and surround the bone and hold it in place, until—"

II

Pat: June 11, 1937–October 12, 2021
Gail: June 18, 1937–

We became best friends in second grade and for seventy-seven years we talked, lost touch, reunited, and continued to talk. In our fifties we began plotting how best to retain our powers into our old age. In our old age we eagerly took up the subject of death.

Both of us were proud of and grateful for the way our lives had turned out. But we adamantly agreed that we would like to receive death's invitation before enough had become enough. Pat confided that she was stealthily collecting her cache of pills and morphine for that day.

My death plans were put on hold for Robert, thirteen years older, whose heart was failing and whose doctor had given him a window of three years to survive his multiple myeloma. Since our midlife courtship, death had been one of our frequent topics. I first wrote "favorite topics," which it was, but didn't want to sound ghoulish, which it wasn't. Although Robert said I was more of a Thanatos person than an Eros, he always got to be the one who went first. We would sit on either side of the fireplace, drinks in hand, and I would say, "I could never stay on in this house without you." And here I am twenty-one years later.

Robert's doctor had predeceased him by two years.

In her late seventies, Pat had a falling off. First a grueling bout of pneumonia. Her lungs were never the same. She had retired from teaching college. When I gave a reading in a town near her, she sent a former student to convey her regrets and ask me to sign a book for her.

A friend reported he had taken her to her favorite restaurant, the International House of Pancakes. She was sharp and witty, he said, and now traveled with a snappy oxygen tank on wheels.

We continued to write letters (by mail; she wouldn't go on the internet) and talk on the telephone. Her hand shook and her printing was almost illegible. I printed my missives back (my handsome cursive was not what it once was), and I often sent a drawing in watercolor pencils.

She sent me a suicide-update poem. It is titled "Cowardly." In the first stanza she is age twelve and climbing the ladder to the high board at the swimming pool. She gets to the top of the ladder, looks down at the water, and backs down. In the second stanza she is forty-four and climbing the steps of the Eiffel Tower. She doesn't quite reach the top when she knows she must go back down. She retreats, murmuring, "Pardon, pardon, pardon . . ." to the climbers she is inconveniencing. In the third stanza, she is eighty-one, and surveys the cache that she has diligently amassed. She lays everything out. She knows what she needs to do. The poem ends

> I called for help
> > Instead.
> > > Now I have to teach
> > > > Myself
> How to climb down
> > Into my death

Yesterday after a visit to the neurosurgeon's office, I found myself in Pat's third stanza. Although I hadn't diligently amassed any going-outers, I calculated the amounts I would have needed. When I was writing my novel *Grief Cottage*, I asked a doctor friend how many painkillers a normal-sized eleven-year-old boy would need to kill himself. She took a long time to calculate and then revised herself, adding a few extra. (I won't report the number.) I thought of the people who would be hurt if I chose this exit. Most of them were already dead, but there were the younger ones. Then I overheard someone saying, "She killed herself." "Oh, no! Was she terminally ill?" "No, she just couldn't face the losing, the dwindling . . ." "Well, I'm surprised. Her heroines were stronger. I probably won't read her again."

The neurosurgeon's waiting room had a big Ingres reproduction of Napoleon dressed as the pope. On a small table by the window were a stack of holy cards and some little wooden crosses.

"All the pictures show no change," he told me.

"None at all?"

"None. In fact, the earlier C-scan was better. In this new one, the break has widened."

Pat called. "Well, I've done it," she said.

For several years, she'd worked it out, set about it, and now it was accomplished.

"Now I own two nightgowns."

After all the legal paperwork, interviews, and bouts of rage at the incompetence of those who stood between her and her goal, she had finally divested herself. She had been giving away her money for years. She signed over her house to the woman who had shopped and cleaned for her.

Now Pat was eligible for Medicaid!

She went by ambulance, accompanied by two devoted ex-students, Greg and "little Pat," and her younger sister, to a small mountain town founded in 1834 by a naval hero of the War of 1812. The inscription on his pedestal in the town square reads, "He Guarded Well Our Seas, Let Our Mountains Honor Him."

Pat's entourage zipped along the new four-lane highway, completed as recently as 2012, and took an uphill right into a lovely little town built to a scale that (so far) has kept anyone from ruining it.

She moved into a double room at the Smoky Ridge nursing home. There was a mature deciduous tree outside her window. No roommate as yet. We said you must have your own room. Days after, the two faithful students and I calculated the expense. One single room would cost us each nine thousand dollars a year. Oh, and she would need an iPad and an iPhone. They would teach her to use these devices.

She declined all offers. She said she had spent her life living inside the gates of privilege. Now she would live outside the gates. Almost a year would pass before she graciously accepted the gift of a telephone by her bed.

Soon a roommate moved in. Blessings. Another person who did not want a TV in the room!

She had the tree in its progress of seasons. Students and friends visited. She talked on the phone to me, preferring the hour before dinner. Her voice-rhythms hadn't changed since childhood. Still the same teacherly tempo. The ironic tilt. The confident, older-sisterly pronouncements. "Pat was born an adult," Pat's mother told mine.

The family story she recounted in her New Year's letter of 1979 ("Dear Gail, last year did not go as planned . . .") set me on the road to my share of fame and fortune.

"You must WRITE this!" I urged her.

"No, you can have it. I'm finished with the nuclear family."

It was now January 1982. Back in Asheville, Pat's mother gave a champagne breakfast so friends could watch me being interviewed by Jane Pauley on the *Today* show.

I wore a sweater with wide red and navy stripes, an olive-green skirt cut on the bias, and the painful expensive shoes I had purchased the day before. The shoes weren't seen because I was behind the desk with Jane.

I had prepared what I was going to say from a phone coaching with the *Today* show booker Emily Boxer, whose large-print, boldfaced questions now lay on the desk below Jane.

("Well, my best friend from childhood sent me a letter in early January of 1979 that began, 'Last year did not go as planned.'")

Some years after, Pat's younger sister told someone who told me: "It would have been fun to sue her."

III

My second night in Kingston Hospital, whose name has recently been changed to Health Alliance. I am nuzzled down deep inside my new hard collar, which must stay on my face and neck for the next six months. It's called an Aspen, fitted earlier in the day by Mr. Brandt.

The neurosurgeon wakes me from sleep, his face looming above mine. ("You're not wearing it correctly! Your chin has to be above the cup. Otherwise it can't do its job.") Under the light from the open door, his hair looks red, a deep cherry red. "You have too many issues to risk surgery. Keep your chin above the cup, not beneath it. Otherwise, it's useless.")

Third day: "A bed has opened up at the nearby rehab center in Lake Katrine, so they'll be sending their van for you later in the day."

After a shockingly bumpy ride in the rehab van, my conveyor unlocks my wheelchair from the van's floor and pushes it onto the exit ramp. Someone who can walk and think and talk like me but has her head in a vise is expected to stay in the wheelchair.

The wing has airy passageways, freshly painted with an attractive design.

"You are going to love your roommate. Elsie is a hundred and one years old and a darling. She used to be a speed skater."

I am introduced to a tiny sylphlike person who was born in 1921. She's in for the long haul, staying in this wing while her permanent roommate recovers from COVID. Circling me on tiptoes, she points to the turned-off TV sets on the wall facing our beds and makes the no, no gesture with her index fingers. "Great," I say. "That's fine with me." Then she indicates her bed with its closed curtains. A head shake: Do not breach. I nod my understanding.

She has the run of the place. Mixes without speaking in the social area with the other patients. When not tiptoeing like a fairy, she covers distances by scuttling along the halls in her wheelchair, propelling herself by her slippered feet. Lots of nice clothes. Frequent changes during the day.

The first night she murmurs behind her curtain. "I think I'm going to die. I think I'm going to die." Plaintive.

Then, alternating through the night, the single ferocious word: "Bitch . . . bitch."

Does she mean me?

The second day she tells a nurse who comes to our room, "She's okay."

That night she stops at the foot of my bed. "Do you want anything?"

The following day she stops at the foot of my bed and beckons me to sit up and come closer. "My father was Russian," she whispers. "My mother was Polish." A pause and a smile, "And I am the little Jewish girl."

Next morning when I return from my workout with the physical therapist, her bed had been stripped. Elsie has been reunited with her roommate.

The curtains are pulled back. An empty space. A wide window that looks out on mowed grass. Should I assert myself and ring for the nurse? ("May I move over to the empty bed by the window? I'll help you move what little stuff I have.") The odd thing is, I only thought of that proactive possibility as I write this now.

The season is moving toward summer solstice, so the room is still light when the night staff replaces the day staff. Members of both staffs roll in a gurney with a large Black woman in red who is telling them a story. It was her foot that brought her to the hospital. She slipped on the stairs and her caregiver panicked and drove her to the emergency room and *dropped* her. "You need to be here," the caregiver said. "It's for your own good."

"She tricked me. She does that when she wants to get her way."

The nurses, a male with a colorful knitted turban and two females, line up her gurney beside the empty bed.

"Can you sit over on the bed, Mrs. B," says the male nurse, "and let's get you out of those clothes."

"I love her but you can't trust her. Years ago, I had an automobile accident. When they pulled me out, my foot was completely separated from my leg. Uh-huh, yes it was. They fixed it but it's never been the same."

She helps them unbutton the red blouse. They unhook her brassiere. "Now if you raise up a little, we'll slip off your skirt."

"Nuh-uh. It's those pee pills. I've gone and done it when you were wheeling me in. It's seeped through the diaper and I'm all wet in back."

"Well, we'll take care of it, Mrs. B. Lift up and let us slip this pad under you and we'll do the rest."

"It's those pee pills. I wish they'd stop giving them to me. As soon as I'm dry, I'm wet again. One of the nurses at the hospital said it's okay if you do it in the diaper. Do the other, too, if you have to. But I didn't like that. To lie in the wet and the poo on top of it, I don't like that."

They think I'm asleep and so haven't drawn the curtain between us. I watch how tenderly the male nurse turns her on her side and lifts up her top leg and expertly slides out the waterproof pad along with the wet diaper and the skirt, which another nurse rescues. She shakes out the pleats and says, "It's just a little damp, we'll hang it up in your locker."

Then the deft sponging and wiping, a fresh diaper, and raising her bottom to slide in a new waterproof pad. The mammoth hip and thigh passively allowing the proficiency of hands to do their job. She has been through this before.

More adjusting, settling in. Mrs. B's medications gone over. "My pee medicine makes me pee in the bed. Next Thursday is my seventy-second birthday. Uh-huh, yes, it is."

One by one they withdraw. Reluctantly. The youngest nurse carrying the pile of wet things. Another removing Mrs. B's wig ("It'll be in your locker") and adjusting her head on two pillows. She is a favorite already. She requires their care. The male nurse in the turban says, "We will get you a larger bed in the morning, Mrs. B."

"Oh, they will have to. I keep slipping over the edge. Is she awake over there?"

I am, and we talk through the night. Mostly Mrs. B, whose name is Agnes Alice, but most people call her Agnes. She asks how I got the neck brace and then repeats the story of her foot that was never the same. "I'm waiting for them to find me a downstairs apartment so I won't have to climb the stairs. I will only have to pay a third of the rent. My caregiver, Brianna, says, 'You've got more money than I do.' She's jealous. I love her but I don't trust her. She keeps four foster children and a baby. She gets seventy-five dollars a week for each of them. When we go out she always wants to go shopping. I said to her, I'm not rich, I have nothing. That's why I get the allotment."

"I'm going to sleep now, Agnes."

"Okay. Nighty-night. My great-granddaughter says, 'Nighty-night. Peek-a-boo.'"

"I love that! Nighty-night. Peek-a-boo."

IV

Pat calls me. It's October, 2018. She's still living in her house.

"My faithful students had it all planned out. They would pick me up and drive me to your talk at the Burnsville literary festival. Afterwards we would announce ourselves and surprise you. I planned it meticulously. The way you plan things while you're still in bed. The hair. The makeup. The outfit. The dress shoes that still looked decent. Then I got the oxygen pack and set it on its wheels. And then I remembered I would have to wear a diaper. And carry a spare one. Would one spare be enough for the drive there and back? And then, forgive me, I made a phone call and went back to sleep."

BURNSVILLE, NORTH CAROLINA
They booked me a year in advance. The invitation had come months earlier. The Carolina Mountains Literary Festival, in its thirteenth year. Held in the high mountain

town of Burnsville, in my home state. I was to be the keynote speaker. I had to sign a contract. They asked for "a talk, not a reading."

This year's theme was "Surface and Rise." Dedicated to people facing a crisis, a challenge, or a life choice. ("We think your novels would be an excellent fit.")

This talk had been building in me for some time. But a few people had to die first. I had known from the beginning I was going to call it "The Desperate Place."

It already had its opening:

> *I can't see a way out of this.*
> *Things will not necessarily get better.*
> *This is my life, but I may not get to do what I want in it.*

"The Desperate Place" examines that place where you find yourself embedded in a situation that is yours alone and that you may be powerless to change.

The festival's artwork was an etching of a writhing ginseng root by a local artist. Reading up on Burnsville and Yancey County, I learned that over eighty-six thousand pounds of the medicinal root had once been processed in this area.

The thirteenth festival was held when the leaves had begun to turn. Burnsville was one of those rare towns that offered no room for expansion. A village square, a courthouse, an old inn famous for its Sunday lunches built by the ginseng merchant Bacchus Smith. The festival rented the inn for one week in September. Sixty years ago I had gone to this silent, sunny little town with a lawyer boyfriend who had business in the courthouse. I waited in the car, reading a magazine interview with Harlan Ellison, feeling the low rumblings of *"I may not get to do what I want."* I desperately wanted to be a writer being interviewed in a magazine, but I was already twenty-five and had published nothing. Now a modern building had taken the place of the old courthouse with columns. The little square across the street, though, was the same.

The festival offered to send a driver to the Charlotte airport so I could fly direct from Albany. My agent, Moses Cardona, arranged for me to have a room in the inn with a walk-in shower, not a tub.

"How did you know to ask for that?"

"Because we just installed a walk-in shower for my mom."

The editor of my journals, Rob Neufeld, got ALS when he was sixty. He was my best reader and champion, and we had phone talks before he lost the power to speak. "You know," he mused, "all my life I have never felt I had enough time to be by myself and read and write as much as I wanted."

Rob edited and wrote commentary for the two volumes of my apprentice journals, *The Making of a Writer,* covering the years 1961–1979, published by Random House in 2006 and 2011.

He spent the first year of his disease drafting the final chapters of a book about my work. I contributed money so he could print a short booklet with selections from the chapters, which we would give away to the people at the Burnsville festival. He and his wife, Bev, came. He sat beside me at a long table after my reading and we signed the booklets for anyone who wanted one. Many people knew him from his historical pieces in the Asheville *Citizen Times*. He was now walking with a cane. As they departed into the evening he stood in the doorway leaning on his cane. "I love you," he called. It was the last time we saw each other.

Rob died a year later. Sunday, October 20, 2019. "Nobody expected it this soon," Bev e-mailed. He had been dedicated to seeing his ordeal through all the way. But early Sunday morning, he woke Bev and said he couldn't breathe.

I realize a part of my work goes with Rob.

I also think a part of me has gone with him. Which part? The part that assures me, "You deserve to be loved and your work remembered."

September 7, 2019

Dear Gail

I am dictating this letter through my friend Bev MacDowell who is writing longhand. Maybe I will have it typed up period. Obviously, you will know what choice I have made.

It has been a long while since we spoke or corresponded for a few reasons. I declined in my capabilities—my physical ones, not my mental ones—but the good news is I have hit a plateau and it has lasted awhile, which gives me hope of a miraculous turn around by which I will have come back from the dead. Watch out world!

I have finally got to read *Old Lovegood Girls* because I have had a good reader. I have been enchanted by your choice to go full bore with your intuitive narrative style and with your thinking about writing as a core experience. I have read 6/7 of the way through so do not yet know in what ways Feron and Merry will find themselves.

My reader is also taking my notes about key themes and plot points. I am paying particular attention to the themes that will go into the remaining four chapters of *The Art of Becoming.* The themes are: fear of the unconscious, empathy, autobiographical writing, and voice. I will also have to add some pieces to completed chapters, for instance Feron's beautiful disquisition about the colors that make up the stages in her life for the chapter, "Self as artist."

Still a little more business to relate. Another friend—like Bev MacD., a member of my book discussion group who have emerged as my major support group—will be helping me get the chapters published as e-books.

You may have had doubts about my ability to be productive because I've had such doubts, but I am feeling invigorated. I often wake up in bed with my hands placed in a certain way on a pillow in my lap and spend an hour or so between first light and breakfast time engaged in relaxed free-ranging thinking. A few things have given me extra motivation.

[The next two paragraphs are private.]

There is another link for you to follow, if you dare. Search for WLOS-TV and on the local station's web site, search for Neufeld. Go to the end of the video and you will see a segment about my receipt of the award for Outstanding Achievement from the WNC Historical Association. The shocking part will be the picture of my debilitation: pillow propped head, wheelchair, ventilator mask, and funny voice. However, people say it's inspiring. They also say, "How could we not have given you this before?"

There is so much ground to cover and so many good stories I wish I could share with you. My God, what a rich life!

How much of your life is not going into your writing? I wish I could transmigrate to a fantasy Rob to which you also come and we would have a time within time. I am working on it. There are indeed some mental or mystical achievements I hope to realize.

I can't promise I will continue to send you long hand letters, but maybe so. Bev MacD. teaches cursive writing at Carolina Day School and we may take advantage of that gift.

Closing with more to disclose,

Love,
Rob

V

Hello. I thought it would be you. I'm seventy-two today. I know you know. I want you to know I know. What time you coming? Who all is coming? Oh, I'll be there. It's a nice place. I can't say that about all the staff. I have a nice roommate. She's a good person. She's a little older than me. But our parents always taught us to be nice to older people. I try to help her out when I can.

That was my son. The oldest one. He owns three houses in Lake Katrine. He won a lawsuit and bought these three houses. He's fixing them up so he can rent them. I have three sons. One holding my hand. One on the hip and one in the stomach. The one holding my hand was four. I said, I need your help to take care of these babies. Oh, he was right on the job.

Here, let's get that poo-poo cleaned up.
Now you stay here and don't move till I come back.
Take that thing out of your mouth. Ooh, nasty.

I loved hearing him bossing his little brothers. And he knew I loved it. That's why he keeps doing it right up to this day. Now he bosses me, too.

You slept a little, Gail. Yes, you did.
Did you snore? Just a little.
("Just a little," Robert used to say.)

This morning, my breakfast tray was minus a teabag. I slid out of bed and set off down the hall to see what I could do. All the nurses were busy. Suddenly "my" nurse darted out of a room. "You! Get back in bed. What are you doing? You want to fall and break your neck a second time?"

Agnes: "She had no business talking to you that way. [Mimics nurse] 'You get back in bed! You want to fall and break your neck a second time?' This is a nice place, but I can't say the same about some of the staff."

"When I get my ground floor apartment I only have to pay a third of the rent. I'm gonna lose some weight and get some new clothes. You won't know me I'll look so good. And I'm gonna have this ring removed from my lip."

It's a gold ring. The size of, well, make a circle with your thumb and middle finger. That size, penetrating the middle of her lower lip. I must have noticed it when they brought her in on the gurney, but then forgot until I noticed it again.

Agnes's tact. It feels like it's inborn. We never discussed TV rules. But from the very first she'd had her set turned at an angle so she could see it without my seeing it. She watches without sound.

There's a preacher she likes. "He won a Grammy. Yes, he did. Maybe I'll turn it up just a little if you don't mind. I love him, but I'm not in love with him. Now I'm only in love with the Holy Spirit."

Her other favorites are *My 600-Lb. Life*, ("I like it because it makes me feel good"), *My Feet Are Killing Me*, and *Dr. Pimple Popper*.

I ended up watching *My 600-Lb. Life* from my side angle. I had never seen someone eating from a plate while driving a car. She was being filmed by someone in the passenger seat. She looks complacent, in charge. We meet the husband, not fat, and the daughter, fat.

The doctor tells her she must lose one hundred pounds before he will consider the surgery. We watch all of it. Bad ending. He threatens to turn her down. She quits. She can't live the rest of her life this way. We see her eating while driving again, looking at peace and in charge.

The patient's spectral appearance made me think of her as the Wraith. She's another of those long-term stayers at the rehab facility. Like my first roommate, Elsie, she spends hours silently present among the others in the dayroom. She is white as a ghost. Her white hair is cut at shoulder length and floats because it's so soft. Right now she's admiring her feet, stretched out in front of her. She's just had a pedicure. What beautiful feet. Nails painted a pale shell pink.

Like Elsie, she whizzes herself to her destinations in her wheelchair, only she stays barefoot.

It's the wee hours in the wing. No staff to be seen or heard in the halls. The Edith Wharton stories of women alone in bed. The servants don't come. Where are they? She doesn't understand. It turns out they are all out at a witches' meeting.

A woman in bed rings and rings. Why doesn't her faithful servant come? This has never happened before. In this story she has just died and doesn't realize it yet.

Agnes and I were talking softly in the darkness.

"I'll tell you where they are. All off together in this place they go to. Smoking dope. Uh-huh."

Suddenly a white figure materializes in the doorway. The Wraith in her wheelchair.

Slowly and deliberately she propels herself forward. Past my bed without giving me a glance. She stops at the foot of Agnes's bed. Does something to Agnes's bare feet sticking outside the covers. Then on to the window, where she takes a hard right to where Agnes's underwear and diapers are stacked next to the bed.

"Gail, ring for the nurse."

"I already have."

The Wraith is transferring Agnes's stack into her own lap.

Agnes: "Stop! Those are my things."

Transfer continues.

"Gail, ring for the nurse again."

"I'm putting on my socks, I'm going to get someone."

"First she plays with my toes, then she steals my clothes."

Agnes's birthday was Thursday, mine on Saturday. "Look at all those flowers. I wish somebody would send me flowers."

"Well, we're going to have a beauty contest and pick the winner and put it on our windowsill and the rest will go home with Jolanta. There are too many. They cancel one another out."

The prize went to Carrie, my sort of goddaughter. She had also sent a box of chocolate truffles ("These are for the staff, so they'll treat you right"). The box never left our room.

"You've got to remember it wasn't just for my birthday, Agnes. Breaking my neck was what brought most of the flowers."

"You heard what that nurse said? 'I had to *wrestle* her to get your things back.' Uh-huh, that what she said. And I told the nurse, 'She was also playing with my toes.' Yes, she was."

The Wraith came a second time. We were waiting for her. So was the nurse. Perhaps sensing she was being followed, the Wraith whizzed past Agnes's toes without a glance. On to the stack of clothes! She had achieved her first transfer before the nurse caught up with her.

"No, dear. Let's put those back."

Again the wrestle. "BUT THEY'RE MINE!" Heard for the first time, the eerie-high voice.

"No, dear, they belong to that lady."

The caught thief is wheeled away.

Evie and Jolanta have just left. Evie brought us a pizza, which I walked over, slice by slice, to Agnes's bed. She sat with her back to us, looking out the window. "Thank you," she said formally each time.

Jolanta brought us some cut grapes and watermelon, and fresh pajamas for me.

"I wish I had nice friends like you."

"Well, yes, they are. Evie is my therapist and we became friends. Jolanta is my personal assistant. She takes care of business at the house."

"Does that make Brianna my personal assistant?"

"I think it does, yes."

"You know, she hasn't gone away."

"Who?" I asked.

"The one who played with my toes and tried to make away with my things. She just goes to a different room, right across the hall, when another nurse is on duty."

"How do you know that?"

"She comes in the afternoon when you take your afternoon nap."

"To that nasty man who drove away his roommate?"

"Uh-huh. They smoke dope together."

"How do you know that?"

"'Cause he stands in his doorway and signals her. Like this."

Agnes makes as if she's smoking dope.

VI

The Desperate Place

*[De-esperare; de = reverse the action of;
esperare = hope]*

I can't see a way out of this.

Things will not necessarily get better.

This is my life, but I may not get to do what I want in it.

I have been close to people who one day found themselves in the desperate place and didn't make it out. *I can't
see a way out of this.*

This will not necessarily get better.
This is my life, but I may not get to do what I want in it.
This is the language that speaks to you in the desperate place.
A place from which you lack the means or power to escape.
A place in which you realize that someone you love does not, and will not ever, love you back.
A place in which you acknowledge your steep falling off in health, or strength, or status. A place in which you must accept that you are losing ground, losing face.

I remember struggling to write a letter to a young man whose father had just hanged himself. The father had been the builder of our house. He was charming and talented and proud of his son. I wrote these things to the son and then came the point in the letter where I was supposed to write something hopeful for the future. All I could think of to convey was *No, you'll never get over it, but the time will come when you will be glad you can't get over it because the loved one remains alive in your heart as you continue to engage with the who and the why of him.*

Two people in my family didn't make it out of their desperate place. My father and my brother.

Though I had seen him only twice when I was a child, I sent my father an invitation to my high school graduation. Mother said not to expect him to show up, but he did. He and his new wife and his brother drove from

Smithfield, North Carolina, to Portsmouth, Virginia, for the ceremony. In the early summer weeks to follow, we wrote letters to each other. He had elegant handwriting and prose to match. He wrote that he would like more than anything to get to know me better. Could I, would it be possible for me to spend a few weeks with them this summer at the beach? I was in my first desperate place at that time and decided to tell him about it—though not all of it. I ended up going to the beach and returning with them to Smithfield and entering Peace Junior College in the fall, paid for by my father.

My father had been doing some personal bookkeeping of his own. At the age of fifty, he had at last achieved a measure of stability. Finally, after thirty years of intemperate living he had managed to stop drinking, had married a new widow in town with a prosperous brother-in-law, and was manager of sales at the brother-in-law's car dealership. For years he had envied his older brother the judge, whose profession gave him status and power and backslapping lunches with lawyers and businessmen, not to mention the stagelike gratification of being the calm character of authority who held sway over messier lives. My father confided to me during the weeks we spent at his brother-in-law's beach cottage that he regretted not having made more of himself. "You mustn't let it happen to you," he said. "Nobody is prepared for how quickly time passes, and you don't want to be one of those people who wakes up in the late afternoon with nothing to show for it." But later, in a radiant moment while we were lying on the beach working on our tans, he told me that I had come along at just the right time, and if he continued to win his battle against depression and alcohol, and if automobile sales continued like this, well, the future didn't look so hopeless after all.

As we lay side by side, congratulating ourselves for finding each other, I had no idea that old disappointments were biding their time, stealthily building like waves, which in less than three years would drown him. One winter afternoon when I was a junior at Chapel Hill, he phoned his brother at his office. "Just felt like saying hello, old son," he said. "Son" was what the brothers called each other. After he hung up, he lay down on the floor of his bedroom in Smithfield and shot himself in the head.

Losing ground. Was that the thing that ultimately killed him? In his twenties, he began losing jobs, losing status, but always got back on his feet. A charming, handsome man, he did not need to keep a steady job as long as his mother was alive. And after her death there would be other admirers waiting in line for whom his looks and charm were enough. By the time he met my mother he was an alcoholic. After that came the mental disorders, given different psychiatric names as the years went by. Once after he had been under treatment, he stopped by to see me at Chapel Hill. He was in a good mood. He had risen again. Smiling, he rummaged in his jacket pocket and pulled out a piece of paper he had torn off a pack of cigarettes. "Here," he said with a laugh. "This is what they said I am this time. I wrote it down." He handed it over and I read in his elegant handwriting, "Psychoneurotic, with compulsion to drink."

When they had been driving back to Smithfield after my high school graduation, he had come down with a raging toothache. They found a dentist along the road who pulled the tooth. But the pain continued and when they got home his dentist told him it had been the wrong tooth. "I should have known," he would finish this story, laughing. "I should have known when we drove into the parking lot and his shingle read: Doctor Payne."

He still had the charm but the looks were going.

This is from a June 16, 2018, *New York Times* opinion piece, "What Kept Me from Killing Myself," by Iraq War veteran Kevin Powers.

"Throughout that summer and into the fall . . . just below the surface of my semi-consciousness, was the constant thought: Maybe I won't wake up this time."

Powers continues, "I doubt much needs to be said about the kind of despair that would make such an idea a source of comfort, despair that came not from accepting that things were as bad as they were going to get, but worse, that they might go on like that forever. The next step felt both logical and inevitable."

Which sounds along the lines of what my twenty-eight-year-old brother might have been thinking in the hours that led up to his death.

In the last week of his life, Tommy was working on a long poem. He left behind two drafts. He titled one "Why Not Just Leave It Alone?" He titled the other "Why Change the World?" One line is the same in both drafts. "My pride is broken since my lover's gone." Both drafts end with the same image of the poet being laid to rest in his wooden home, "With my trooper hat on my chest bone."

He was my half brother, but why quibble about the half when he and I kicked and floated, eighteen years apart, in the same watery womb and grew to the rhythms of the same mother's heart?

It was October 2, 1983. October 1 was our mother's birthday, which is why I was in North Carolina: She liked all her children to be there for her birthday. I flew down from New York; my half sister, Franchelle, drove up from Columbia with her family; my half brother Rebel drove across the state from Chapel Hill. I wrote about this in my novel *A Southern Family*. Tommy became Theo, a name that would have suited him. Rebel became Rafe. I chose the name Clare for myself because I hoped for more clarity. There is no younger sister in *A Southern Family* because—once again, why quibble about the half?—my sister, who is an attorney, told me after the publication of *The Odd Woman* that she would rather be excused from serving for any characters in my future novels.

What happened, what we know happened, as opposed to all that we can never know, was that on the Sunday afternoon after Mother's Saturday birthday, Tommy, who had just turned twenty-eight, ironed a shirt at his parents' house, where he had been living with his three-year-old son. He told Mother he was going over to see J., the woman he loved, a nurse, who also had a three-year-old son. They had planned to marry, they had even made out a budget. Then J. suddenly broke it off. Tommy told Mother he was going over to ask J. to reconsider. "I'm going to settle it one way or another before the afternoon is out," he said, and drove off alone.

COUPLE FOUND SHOT was the headline in the newspaper next morning. Afterward, we would go over and over it. My stepfather would hire a detective. The police report would be taken out of the files again and again and scrutinized: Maybe we would see something new that we had missed before. "The real truth" would suddenly reveal itself on some overlooked line in the official text. "The real truth" being something everybody could bear.

This much we knew. Tommy, J., and J.'s three-year-old son were in J.'s car. The child was in the back seat. The car pulled over on a shady residential street. A boy riding his bicycle saw two people arguing inside the car. Shots were fired. A neighbor called the police. When they arrived, the woman lay on the street on the passenger's side of the car. She was already dead. The man was unconscious and writhing on the ground on the driver's side. A .25-caliber Belgian semiautomatic lay on the front seat of the car. J.'s son was found uninjured in the back seat.

Tommy had his own pistols. He belonged to the National Rifle Association. He won prizes for marksmanship. But this particular pistol belonged to his father, Frank. He and Frank had lent it to J. several weeks before to keep in her glove compartment because she said a man had been stalking her. J. had been in the army and knew how to shoot, too.

The day before, on Mother's birthday, I knew Tommy was unhappy. But Tommy was always unhappy. He "felt things more than most," was the family euphemism for his troubled nature. He took most to heart the family's fractures as well as the world's. Drawing you in with his shy, closemouthed smile, he would offer his latest tale of woe. But always, always before in his stories, there had been a quality of suspense, of entertainment. He starred in them as the knight-errant, complete with pratfalls and setbacks, but a knight-errant who picked himself up, dusted himself off, and set out on his next mission. Tommy was a modern Samaritan who carried a first aid kit and a blue flasher in his car in case he came across an accident. He had wanted to become a state trooper, but even the state troopers he hung around with urged him to get a college education first and "then see." So he went to college and became an accountant. Weeks before his death, he had applied for a job with the IRS. He was sick and tired of helping boring business people keep more of their money, he said; he wanted the high drama of catching the cheaters.

The afternoon before his death, on my mother's birthday, we were in the kitchen and he told me the story of his girlfriend suddenly breaking off with him. But this time something was different. I was not, as usual, deriving the usual listener's satisfaction from his story. Many years later when remembering that kitchen scene, I realized what had spooked me about it: Not only was there not a trace of the shy, closemouthed smile, there was no knight-errant starring in my brother's story. The tone was new: one of bafflement and resignation. There was no sense of any future missions. There was no tug of suspense. It was like a story that had already happened.

Tommy would be sixty-three now. He was born that same summer that my father drove from Smithfield to Glen Burnie, Maryland, and rescued me from my desperate place. If on that October 2 afternoon twenty-eight years later there had not been a pistol handy in the glove compartment of J.'s car, would Tommy have remarried somebody else and raised his son and reconciled himself to a fallen world as long as he had a first aid kit and a job that gave him satisfaction that he was rescuing people from injustices?

But now, I do hear his voice, the old Tommy voice, just as it was in life, chiding me as he defends the position of his beloved National Rifle Association with its singsong refrain: "Gail, guns don't kill people, people do."

During the winter following Tommy's death, I had an awful dream. I awakened with my heart thudding and it took a minute to remember who I was and a few more minutes for the rage and hopelessness to drain out of me. It was unlike any dream I'd ever had. There was no action in it. There were no visuals. I didn't see anything or hear anything. I was in the black box of myself and felt only pure, stark emotion. I wanted to die, or kill somebody, OR BOTH, because this person didn't love me. The person was genderless. I was genderless. It was just the unbearable agony of knowing myself NOT LOVED and wanting to kill/die to avenge myself and put an end to the pain. After I had calmed down, I lay in bed and thought: that would be just like Tommy to find a posthumous way to hand over this dream like a neat, well-wrapped package: "Here you go, Gail. Feel my pain."

When we left the twenty-five-year-old Iraq veteran Kevin Powers, he had plunked down the last of his army pay on a year's rent for a small apartment, kept the shades down and the door locked except for his daily trip to the 7-Eleven store for a case of beer, two packs of cigarettes, and two big bite hot dogs. He spent six months of 2005 drunk. "And yet," he tells us, "I'm here writing this almost 13 years later, despite the fact that in the perpetual semidarkness of that Richmond apartment, I wanted to not be, wanted to not be with an intensity that very few desires in my subsequent life have equaled."

He got so he couldn't read. His hand trembled and he kept one eye closed. Then, for some reason, he picked up *The Collected Poems of Dylan Thomas* and opened to the first page, on which the poet offers the reader his poems "with all their crudities, doubts, and confusions." For the first time, Powers recognized himself in another person. ("Nothing came as close to characterizing what my life had become as those three words ['crudities,' 'doubts,' and 'confusions'] . . . and somehow that simple tether allowed me to slowly pull myself away from one of the most terrifying beliefs common to the kind of ailment I'm describing: that one is utterly alone, uniquely so, and that this condition is permanent.")

Over the next several years Kevin Powers read more books, went to college, courtesy of the army, and began to write poetry and fiction. In 2012 he published a celebrated war novel, *The Yellow Birds*. Next he took on the horrors of the Civil War: *A Shout in the Ruins* was published in 2018. He also wrote a book of poems, *Letter Composed During a Lull in Fighting.*

Just as I continue to engage with the who and the why of my father and my brother, I also ask myself, What small detail might have made the difference in Kevin Powers's case? It works both ways. What if he hadn't happened to pick up that Dylan Thomas collection, or opened to those three words: "crudities," "doubts," and "confusions"?

During my life, I have found myself in the desperate place four times. But that first time, at age eighteen, was by far the worst.

Summer 1955. We were living in a tract house in Glen Burnie, Maryland. There were a hundred or so identical houses in the development, which ran alongside a busy highway. Inside our house was my pregnant mother, my two-and-a-half-year-old half sister, my stepfather, who had been transferred by the chain stores he worked for six times in four years. And myself, who had just graduated as salutatorian from Woodrow Wilson High School in Portsmouth, Virginia. Because of my stepfather's many transfers, I had gone to six high schools in four years. Ninth grade at St. Genevieve's, in Asheville,

North Carolina, on a full scholarship that I had to abandon when we left town at the end of ninth grade. Tenth grade in Anderson, South Carolina, where my little sister was born. Eleventh grade split between Norview High in Norfolk, Virginia, and Woodrow Wilson, across the river in Portsmouth. Twelfth grade divided between a first semester at Woodrow Wilson, three weeks in a high school in Louisville, Kentucky, then the last two months at Glen Burnie High School, and back to Woodrow Wilson for graduation.

Now summer was beginning and everybody seemed to have a future but me. My mother was expecting her second child in August. My stepfather was starting over at a new W. T. Grant store, in Baltimore, where he had not yet alienated the boss. That morning I had received a letter from Mother Winters, my mentor at St. Genevieve's. She congratulated me on being salutatorian, asked about my plans for college, and brought me news of some of my classmates. "Pat has won the four-year Angier-Duke scholarship to Duke, Carolyn will be going to Radcliffe, Stuart and Lee to St. Mary's in Raleigh . . ."

Here I stopped reading and felt . . . what? A dry mouth, a pang in the chest, a sense of going down, of losing myself. All I knew to do was mark my position.

My position. At that time I couldn't hold all of it in my mind. If I had tried, I might have despaired, or lashed out and hurt myself or somebody else. I had so little experience to draw from and there was no escape.

> . . . a distinct sense of loss, a flavour in the mouth
> of the real abiding danger that lurks in all the forms
> of human existence.

That is Joseph Conrad describing the sensations of the commander of a stranded ship in *The Mirror of the Sea*. But I had not read Conrad yet, or any of the richly chronicled descriptions in the literature and religions of the world of what it feels like to be in the desperate place.

It would be years before I came across passages in books or met people who described the place in which I was embedded. It would be years more before I began writing books in which people found themselves in the desperate place.

Since my early teens, I had been building my life on false premises. I was creating a persona to meet the requirements of my family's frequent moves. This persona was more extroverted than I. She pretended to more confidence and security than I felt. I became a pro at embellishing and editing my history. When I entered a new school, I "went out" for things I was good at that would bring me attention. The school paper, the drama club, painting posters and scenery, entering competitions—and of course getting high grades. I dated lots of boys, made it a point to be cagey and hard to get until each got fed up and moved on, usually just as I had begun to appreciate him.

That was the outside of things. Inside our various rented domiciles other dramas were playing out. We were not free people. Our embattled breadwinner, who was angry much of the time, sometimes knocked one of us to the floor for challenging him. There was no money for us except what he doled out and no going anywhere he didn't drive us. As I entered my teens, the breadwinner, who was only twelve years older than me, often spoke of how he "loved" me. His voice trembled. At night I would wake to find him kneeling in the dark beside my bed, his hand taking liberties.

My mother had shed her former confident self. As a child, I knew a mother who arrived home on the ten P.M. bus after her wartime job on the newspaper, a woman who taught college and on weekends typed up love stories that earned one hundred dollars apiece. This powerless woman seemed more like someone I was visiting in prison. Only I was in prison with her. She suffered because there was no money to send me to college. She made phone calls to a private college in Baltimore to see if I could go as a day student. The registrar said a partial scholarship might be arranged, given my academic record, but where was the rest of the money to come from? There was no "rest of the money," my stepfather reminded us, as though we were dim-witted. He suggested I take a year off and find a job, "maybe in sales work," and save up for college next year. He added magnanimously that I could continue to live under his roof for the time being without paying rent.

That's the way the ground lay, that 1955 June morning in Glen Burnie, when the girl sat cross-legged on her bed, the letter from her old teacher clutched in her fist. "Pat to Duke, Carolyn to Radcliffe, Stuart and Lee to St. Mary's . . .

> This is my life, but I may not get to do what I want in it.
> I can't see a way out of this.
> Things will not necessarily get better.

In my novel *Unfinished Desires*, about the life of a girls' school, two old nuns are being driven back to their retirement home from doctors' visits, and one says to the other, "There was a sentence this morning in that Prayer for Holy Women: 'In our weakness your power reaches our perfection.' What do you think it means, Sister Paula?" Sister Paula thinks for a minute and then replies, "I think it means you have to fully admit you can't save yourselves before you're fully available to God."

That morning in Glen Burnie, God was undergoing some very slippery changes in my psyche. He had ceased being the attentive heavenly father who was always aware of me, and he had not yet expanded into the mystery beyond my understanding that I am still pursuing today.

All I could be certain of, that long-ago summer morning, was that I could not save myself.

But something else did, something already embedded in the tissue of my particular circumstances: the earthly father who had been the absent father. In a mood of defiant resignation, I decided to send him an invitation to my graduation anyway. Of course he wouldn't come.

But he did come. And when we were lying beside each other on the beach, he said, "When I opened your invitation, after I got over being pleasantly surprised, I thought to myself, Well, this is one thing I did that came to fruition. And then, after we began to write letters to each other, it struck me that I might be the rescuer you needed."

—Talk given to the September 2018 Carolina Mountains Literary Festival

VII

From Pat's friend and former student Greg Lissenbee
Four months after her death

February 20, 2022

Last summer I was alerted by social services that
pretty much all of Pat's "surplus money" had to be
spent immediately and *the money had to be spent on
Pat.* Nursing home billing issues and random
reimbursements due to the pandemic led to some
odd, odd money issues colliding with Medicaid
rules. One thing was for certain: I didn't want her
to lose Medicaid, resulting in both of us having to
wade through another pit of Medicaid application
quicksand.

Pat might have wanted me to use some of that
money to reimburse myself for gasoline, wear and
tear on the car, etc., but that was not an option.

Social Services said the money had to be spent directly for Pat . . . and of course I agreed with that. Given that Pat got somewhat "agitated" about anything involving money, I decided to try to figure out a plan on my own. And honestly it came down to either a plot in a beautiful cemetery or cases and cases and cases (and more cases) of adult diapers. (She was always adamant about not wanting any "luxury items . . . like a TV" in her room.)

I'm grateful that before the deadline of spending the money, I was able to buy a plot—and I was able to prepay the money for the stone.

Shortly after her soul left her body, I went to the gravestone shop and found the one you see in the photo. I thought it was perfect in that it was a heart, of course—and I thought the "marbleized paisley" look—and the roses at the base—very much spoke to more than one of Pat's sensibilities.

Even though I know she had an occasional thought about ashes being scattered in rivers and buried under a tree, I have often felt her smiling down on me and saying, "Thank you, Gregory—I love what you chose." The week before last I took red roses to the spot and said, "Happy Valentine's Day." I miss her so very, very much.

VIII

I am being discharged. It is Thursday, June 30, the last day of my eighty-fifth birthday month.

Jolanta, looking businesslike with her hair in a tight braid this morning, slides the last stack of my personal items from the locker into the overnight bag she has brought. Her obvious satisfaction during this retrieval reminds me of the Wraith's complacence as she transferred Agnes's things into her wheelchair.

Everybody is busy, goodbyes have been said earlier. My acerbic nurse, Roberta, whom I have come to like (yes, the one who shouted, "You! Get back in bed. You want to break your neck a second time?"). My physical therapists, from giant John of Barbados ("Slow down, my friend, slow down") to Kimberly, who amassed five degrees: English, education, Bible studies, then two in physical therapy) before she found her calling. I quizzed her while she was training me how to get around in a simulated kitchen without bending or twisting my neck.

Gail: "Who said, 'Here am I. Send me.' "

Kimberly: "Isaiah. Isaiah 6:8."

I gave Kimberly my email address and asked her to let me know how things were going in her life. She said she would.

"I need a minute," I told Jolanta, "You go on ahead."

I stood beside Agnes's bed, holding her hand. We looked at each other. Then slowly our hands slipped apart.

IX

My discharge did not go as planned. As Jolanta drove us out of the rehabilitation center her cell phone rang.

"Hello? Oh, NO!"

Carrie, my elective goddaughter, would not be coming today to stay with me.

She had COVID.

Now we are home. I have been away since June 6, 2022. Today was June 30.

As we cross the gravel courtyard on foot Jolanta looks balefully at the scraggly little dogwood and asks, "Why couldn't you have waited one more day? You knew I was coming on Tuesday."

"Well, I *didn't* wait."

"I know, I know. What is done is done."

We go up the two stone steps I last crawled up—across the stone porch. Into the house. Take a left. Past the kitchen. Another left into Robert's room. Where he spent the final three years of his life after he could no longer climb stairs.

This will be "Gail's room" now.

For how long?

Would you want to know?

Well, I . . .

Yes or no?

In that case, no.

In this room for three years, Robert sat sideways on the edge of his bed, looked out the window, and said his morning prayer.

"Thank you for letting me live to this day."

The bottle of brandy lying sideways in the top drawer of the bedside table, for sleepless-night swigs.

Until very early one morning, April 21, 2001, when my bedside phone rang upstairs.

I picked up.

"Come down," he said. (His students said, "His voice is lower than God's.")

"The bed is ready," said Jolanta, "or would you rather sit in the chair?"

"Bed."

In six months, when my collar comes off, will I be back in my upstairs room?

The cat is watching behind the sofa.

"Shall I go and get him?"

"No. Let him come when he's ready." He has been alone for a month. Except for Carl, my caretaker, and

Evie and Jolanta, who drop in to feed him and check his litter box.

After leaving the rehab center, we went first to the office of Dr. H., the neurosurgeon.

He was annoyed with the new CT scan. He paced back and forth, flipping his fingers at the report. He was in street clothes. In bright daylight his hair was an unusual magenta color with straggles of gray.

"These are *worse* than the earlier ones. Before, the break was *this* wide. Now it is *this* wide. You have too many issues for surgery. You are going to drink lots of milk, eat ice cream, dairy . . . Take at least ten minutes in the sun every day. Even if the sun's not out. Not in the rain, but overcast will work. Order a new CT scan in three weeks and come back to this office in one month. We'll see if the break is healing. Keep your collar on."

"Even when I'm sleeping?"

"At all times."

"What if it doesn't heal?"

"You'll have to have surgery."

Apocryphal or Disremembered

The apocryphal story of how Pat and I became friends. Second grade. I was frantically trying to get both my legs into one leg of my snowsuit. The school bus was leaving and I was about to miss it. Pat helped me disentangle myself.

I say apocryphal because I'm not sure it happened. Yet over the years when I would tell this story in her presence, she never contradicted it.

I missed the bus and ran after it screaming, "St-o-o-o-p!" The bus stopped and there was much kerfuffle, nuns converging on the scene and exclaiming in French, the language they switched to so we wouldn't understand.

In those days, the 1940s and '50s, two water fountains stood on Pack Square in Asheville, one on either side of the seventy-five-foot granite obelisk memorializing Zebulon Vance. The fountain on the left was for COLORED.

The one on the right was for WHITE. I told Pat that Annie's mother said if she drank out of the COLORED fountain she would turn into a Negro. "How ignorant," said Pat. "Let's go and test it out." When I hung back, she strode ahead, arms swinging. She drank deeply and called, "How do I look now?"

We would have been about ten.

Recently, when I was telling someone how Pat had divested herself and spent her final years in the Smoky Ridge nursing home as the "owner of two nightgowns," I told the Pack Square COLORED and WHITE story. Because I wanted a strong example of the person Pat would grow up to be.

Were Pat and I ever on Pack Square together when we were about ten?

In *A Mother and Two Daughters* I made up other acts of bravery by having "Cate" lead a march to block the Lincoln Tunnel or "Cate" questioning why busloads of imprisoned Japanese Americans were being relocated to Grove Park Inn in Asheville.

Did I *make up* the whole Pack Square incident?

For a while not so long ago, I got obsessed over what Jesus had really said and done.

I ordered all the Jesus Seminar books, in which biblical scholars had made color-coded assessments as to what Jesus really had said or done.

Red sayings and doings were "most probably his."

The pink ones "may have suffered modifications."

The gray ones "did not originate with him but may reflect his ideas."

The black ones were "the results of the storyteller's imagination," in other words "inauthentic."

I made a short list of my favorite Gospel stories. Then I tested them against the scholars' color-coded assessments.

The centurion of great faith in Matthew 8:5, also in Luke 7:1–10, is colored black and assumed to have been created by the storyteller(s).

Jairus's little daughter ("Get up, little girl"), in Mark 5:22–43, Matthew 9:18–25, and Luke 8:41–42, 49–56, was colored black by common consent. ("The words of Jesus are not particularly memorable, are not aphorisms or parables, would not have circulated independently during the oral period, and cannot therefore be traced back to Jesus.")

The passage about the father with the lunatic boy ("If thou canst believe, all things are possible to him that believeth") in Mark 9:17–24, Matthew 17:14–21, and Luke 9:37–43 was colored black. ("The incidental dialogue ascribed to Jesus in this story is the creation of the narrator who is exercising the storyteller's license.")

Now for John 21:1–14 (fishing instructions, breakfast cooked by Jesus on shore, Jesus's third appearance to the disciples after being risen from the dead).

The scholars concluded that "the dialogue assigned to Jesus is the result of the storyteller's imagination. Jesus is made to say what the narrator thinks he might have said on such an occasion."

So many of my favorites colored black!

I realized halfway through the pink that not only was I becoming confused and irate, but I felt I was probably committing some form of Bible abuse. So I shelved the Jesus Seminar volumes among the rest of my religion and psychology books and allowed them some rest.

But what has remained with me from that compulsive exercise was the Seminar's conclusion that Jesus's voice was a distinctive one. And they went on to say why:

His sayings and parables cut against the social and religious grain of the times. They were often characterized by exaggeration, humor, and paradox.

They surprised and shocked.

They frustrated ordinary expectations.

The scholars reaffirmed for me that this was definitely a teacher and preacher worth a lifetime's pursuit.

A teacher kneels on the shore to cook breakfast for his hungry disciples because he loves them. They don't dare say it's their teacher who was crucified, but nevertheless they know it's him.

If I had thought of it, I would have discussed this with my occupational therapist Kimberly at the rehabilitation center.

She would be able to quote chapter and verse. And I can hear us agreeing that the glow from that fire on the shore is still burning bright and that we recognize the teacher in our midst.

> As soon as they were come to land, they saw a fire of coals there, and fish laid thereon, and bread. Jesus saith unto them, Bring of the fish which ye have now caught. Simon Peter went up, and drew the net to land full of great fishes, a hundred and fifty and three: and for all there were so many, yet was not the net broken. Jesus saith unto them, Come and dine. And none of the disciples durst ask him, Who art thou? knowing that it was the Lord. Jesus then cometh, and taketh bread, and giveth them, and fish likewise. This is now the third time that Jesus showed himself to his disciples, after he was risen from the dead.
>
> —John 21:9–14

Pack Square. The Vance monument. Flanked by two fountains, one for COLORED and one for WHITE.

George Pack was a turn-of-the-twentieth-century lumber millionaire who moved to the Asheville mountains for his wife's health. He took up philanthropy, founded a library, Pack Memorial (which at first was only by subscription), and donated the portion of land on top of downtown Asheville: Pack Square.

Zebulon Vance was thrice governor of North Carolina during the Civil War and Reconstruction and later a U.S. senator. His seventy-five-foot granite obelisk monument was completed in 1898 and dominated the square until 2021, when it was taken down block by block. The contractor couldn't use a crane because the underground parking garage at the site couldn't bear the weight of the equipment.

The Vance monument was the third Confederate monument to be removed from Asheville's Pack Square following racial-justice protests after the murder of George Floyd.

Wrote Rob Neufeld, Asheville's historical columnist: "The Vance Obelisk is one of the few Civil War monuments in the South that is an abstract thing. It is not of a person, a soldier, a horse, or an object that symbolizes slavery." Mayor Esther Manheimer said, "This isn't an easy removal like a horse and rider statue where it might happen in the cover of darkness very quickly."

The demolition was halted, however, because of a ruling from the court of appeals on June 4, 2021, and it took until 2022 for the state supreme court to reverse the ruling and allow the removal to continue. It was reported that the stone blocks of the monument were to be disposed of so that it could not be re-created somewhere in the future. But on August 14, 2023, the state supreme court announced it would hear arguments on a new case on November 1, 2023. The plaintiffs, the Society for the Historical Preservation of the 26th Regiment North Carolina Troops, are seeking to save the stones and maybe rebuild the monument.

Citing a 2015 donation agreement between the society and the city for the successful restoration financed by $140,000 of donations from individual members, attorney Edward Phillips III says he's cautiously optimistic that the city will have to rebuild the monument, most likely at its former site.

However, Asheville City Attorney Brad Branham says he sees the court date as a "procedural one." There's always the option to ask for oral arguments versus simply deciding over written briefs.

The plaintiffs argue that while Vance owned six slaves and was known for his strong support of slavery, he was still a great man. He was in the 26th Regiment.

On September 26, I emailed the Asheville attorney to ask if there were any new developments. He wrote back, "As you said the case is scheduled for oral arguments at the N.C. Supreme Court on November 1st. A decision won't likely come for some time thereafter. Until at least that time, the removed materials will remain securely stored."

If Rob Neufeld and Pat were still around to have a conversation, I can imagine how it might have gone: with Rob, who grew up in New Jersey and became a reporter for the *Citizen Times*; and Pat, who at age ten drank out of the COLORED fountain and called to me triumphantly; "How do I look now?" and myself, who went with her mother to visit the Zebulon Vance memorial homestead, who late in life named her cat "Zeb," and who now, even later in life, agrees with Oralene Simmons and the Vance Monument Task Force, which recommended the monument's removal.

The first Black person to integrate Mars Hill College, where Pat was a professor of English for fifty years, Oralene Simmons said she would have no problem with the monument, or its stones, being displayed in a museum where people wanted to see it, but "it would really be a step back, which is really out of step with today's times. I think it would reopen old wounds, and it would call people to action." (Quoted in John Boyle's "Let's Hope the Vance Monument Stays in a Warehouse," Asheville Watchdog, August 14, 2023.)

XI

Pat's winter solstice letter—undated—before she moved to Smoky Ridge nursing home.

Dear Gail,

I think of you when the light grows sullen and scant. I send extra blessings hoping that more darkness can lead you to more dreaming.

I feel that I am dwelling in another world already. It is rich with memories of all the places and all the men and our long friendship. The trees around my house greet me daily, and I them. My cat Phoebe is more soft and confiding than my boyfriend ever troubled himself to be.

And if there is another life—fantasies of the next time fascinate me. But if there is no other, to merge with the air and the earth would be an honor too. I wish I knew how to persuade my strong, strong body that this dance is over. She's still looking for partners—"Hi! Wanna play?"

If you find the crack between the two worlds, please let me know. Otherwise, I'll find it and meet you there with love. Who knows?

I love you

Pat

XII

April 15, 2023

Dear Pat,

It's after your death that I'm answering your undated letter, the one beginning "I think of you when the light grows sullen and scant."

As recently as yesterday, new greenery is popping up outside the windows of this house. I fell on the gravel last June 6 and broke my neck and spent the rest of June 2022 in hospital and rehab. Since then I have moved down to Robert's room, which began as our guest room, the place you always slept when you were visiting. So much to report! You write, "If you find the crack between the two worlds, please let me know."

Time travel is a reality if you're in the right frame of mind. And I seem to have wedged myself into the crack you mentioned in your undated letter written before you gave away your money and house and transmuted yourself to Smoky Ridge.

Too many ideas to catch and hold. This is the countdown to April 22, Robert's "year's mind." It will now be twenty-two years here by myself in this house. "Year's mind" went out of popular use five centuries ago, but the phrase still survives in the Episcopal Liturgy. "We remember Robert Starer, whose year's mind falls on this day" (April 22). "We remember Pat Verhulst, whose year's mind falls on this day" (October 12).

"Year's mind" means the day of one's death.

I'm wondering if I can employ some sort of *compressed narrative summary* to fill you in on my ordeal/adventure of the past year. This may not work. But why not try?

Okay. Went out to water a little dogwood, lost my balance, fell face forward on the gravel court-yard and broke my neck. (The "C-2 bone," which is also known as "the hangman's break.")

In the hospital, the local neurosurgeon said, "You have too many issues for surgery," and convinced me I should play safe and "sit quiet for six months" until C-2 had a chance to heal by itself. I was old, but old bones could heal. My regimen was to be on lots of milk and dairy, at least ten minutes in the sun daily, and a hard collar to keep the neck from moving forward or backward. He had ordered an Aspen Vista cervical collar in my size and the representative would bring mine to the hospital the next day. It was to be worn at all times, even for sleeping. Get a CT scan every month and schedule an office visit every month.

There was also a prescribed calcitonin salmon nasal spray to be used daily in alternate nostrils.

This isn't starting off very compressed. Let's fast-forward seven months:

"This has happened only three times in my thirty years of practice," said the neurosurgeon. "I would like to send you to the surgeons at Westchester. I know them. I trust them. I want you to live."

And so began Part II of my ordeal/adventure. In early February of 2023, Dr. A., the super-surgeon, cut open my neck and, with another super-surgeon, fused C-2 (the hangman's bone) with C-1 and C-3 and sewed and stapled me up.

Fast-forward to April 16, 2023:

So here am I, home in Robert's downstairs bedroom for his final three years. Rusa, my long-term health care person, has set me up with my bed table, and my three brown leather notebooks containing my year's work on *Getting to Know Death: A Meditation*, begun seriously on August 10, 2022.

After a quote from Arthur C. Clarke's *Childhood's End* ("No intelligent person resents the inevitable") I make it official:

This is the day after August 9, 2022, the day I chose to mark the months of the accepted inevitable and to fill them honorably after depressing visit to the neurosurgeon ("This CT scan shows no change").

This was my euphemistic way of announcing the dark intent underneath. ("Okay, I'll write *Getting to Know* during these six months of bondage. When this cervical collar comes off, depending on the outcome, I'll choose whether to go on living or start planning how to snuff myself out.")

You've been here, remember? You collected your stash of snuffing-outers, and then when you couldn't go through with it, you wrote your "Cowardly" poem, which ends

> I called for help
> instead.
> Now I have to teach myself
> how to climb down
> > into my death.

> Rusa?
> Ye-e-s.
> Will you bring me a cup of coffee?
> Of course I will.

My headache is better than when I woke. But it's still there. When my super-surgeon phoned from Westchester last week, he was disappointed about the headaches I reported. He sent me for a CT scan. ("We've got to find out what this is.") My instructions were to wear a soft collar for a while. I ordered three from Amazon.

It's better to write with a headache than lie still and think about my headache.

"I am dismayed when I'm not writing, completely content when I am." John Le Carré told a *New York Times* interviewer a few months before his death.

Here's a conundrum.

If I hadn't broken my neck, I would never have known someone like Agnes, Mrs. B., my roommate at the rehab center.

If I hadn't broken my neck, I would never have known someone like Rusa.

Does that mean you are glad to have broken your neck?

No, no, no.

"Then what?"

"I don't know." I just know I am glad to know Agnes and Rusa.

By the way, just to check things out I consulted journals from 2020 and 2021. Back then I walked with a cane for bad balance. I entertained scenarios of snuffing myself out. I spent some days in bed. I fell down the steps and once on the bathroom floor.

Euphemism—from the Greek for "good speech."

Synonyms: inoffensive ("passed away" vs. "died")

substitution

doublespeak

weasel word

Am I "climbing down into my death"?

XIII

Still to Pat, after your death:

Rusa has been a home health care person in this country for twenty-four years. She is from Georgia— the one next to Russia. She is named after Queen Rusudan from the thirteenth century. "Our queen was very successful. She made our country bigger by taking other countries. But then the Mongols came. Disaster!"

In Georgia, Rusa was a journalist, linguist, and teacher. After her mother died and Georgia got a corrupt leader, she came to America with her daughter. Her husband was not allowed to join the family. "So I talked to him every day for ten years and one day he said he did not want to go on with this. He said he was too lonely." Now her daughter is married with two sons. She lives in Georgia. In Atlanta.

Rusa looks about forty, but she is sixty-six. She takes care of herself. She has perfect pink skin and cuts and colors her own hair. "Every time I would go to the hairdresser I would come home crying. She never did what I wanted. I also was crying for the three hundred dollars."

At the moment Arik, the physical therapist, is working with me to climb stairs. ("Slowly, slowly. Why are you in a hurry?") When I finally achieve the twenty-four stairs, he makes me sit down in my old room, with all the windows and all the sunrises and moonrises. "Catch your breath," he says.

Rusa sleeps here now. I look around. She has made changes. Several "serious" mirrors. Many cosmetics. She asked for a new shower in the bathroom because the old one stopped working even before Robert died. She keeps the windows closed and the blinds down. ("I am frightened. Something outside in the night.") Yet she has tracked a young bear with her iPhone camera from indoors as he leisurely traipsed across the grass in front of the house and then returned to the woods. She ordered a device that massages her feet and has asked my permission to order an indoor exercise bike.

She has all the hairdresser's tools and now cuts my hair and blow-dries it.

She cooks. Her last job was with a lady who never wanted to eat the same meal twice. Rusa gained thirty pounds, which she's trying to lose.

Her longest job lasted seven years. She took care of Michael, in his nineties, until his death at 101. She still cries for him.

She is a licensed home health care person. On her weekends off (every other one) she is replaced by Natia, thirty-one, also from Georgia. Natia is very tall and very beautiful, with not much English. But she told Rusa she likes it here because it's peaceful. Natia has a degree in Georgian law. Her five-year-old son, Luca, lives with her mother in Georgia.

Rusa said only fourteen countries in the world have their own alphabet. Georgia is one of those fourteen countries.

Her English is higher pitched than when she talks in Georgian with her daughter in Atlanta. It has a lilt and some strange pronunciations of words she met first in print.

She is a ceaseless storyteller. I have to say, "Stop, stop! That's too much."

"You think I talk too much?"

"I need time to think about what you already said."

★ ★ ★

Worrisome aspects of my life. Money and health.

In the last years of my mother's life (age seventy-two to seventy-seven) she said frequently, "I hope I don't outlive my money." And we would counter: "Oh, we hope you do."

But she was driving to the airport to pick up Rebel, her thirty-one-year-old "little boy" when she apparently suffered a heart attack. Her car crossed the grassy median and hit a car going in the opposite direction. The driver of that car broke both legs. He was a mural painter. His wife had to have plastic surgery on her face. Their dog ran away from the accident but was later found.

She had not outlived her money. My sister Franchelle and my brother Rebel and I divided what was left. Her obituary said she was seventy-two, but she was seventy-seven. She had been changing the age on her driver's license for years.

Now I am saying to myself, "I hope I don't outlive my money."

Thanks to your family story ("Last year did not go as planned") that set me on the path to fortune, I have been able to live in this house on the hill and write for forty-one years.

At my eightieth birthday party, I quoted lines from Psalm 16 ("My lines have fallen in pleasant places"), but a year ago, about the time I broke my neck, I saw my bounty dwindle. Steps must be taken.

So I call Willard and he sets up an HECM (home equity conversion mortgage), insured by the federal government, which allows me to stay put in this house.

Robert named our house Villa Godstar. We also called it "the castle" and "the orphanage."

Forty-one years ago John Irving generously referred me to Willard Saperston, a former English student of his. Willard now had his own asset management company. When John's fortunes suddenly soared, Willard visited him in his writing shed in Vermont and offered his services. John asked him if he would patch his shed roof with tar while he finished his day's writing. Afterward they made an agreement that endures to this day. Willard's daughter Kristina is now his business partner.

The actuaries predict I have ten more years.

During that ten years, more damage and disintegration has to be taken into account.

Do you care to imagine the particulars of that disintegration?

Not now.

So much for money. Now, about worrisome health. Up until last year my "breaks" were limited to three instances of broken feet and one compression fracture in the lower spine. The broken neck was my passport to seven months in a vise and my first serious surgery, followed by two months (so far) of pain.

Which brings me back to Rusa.

She comes to me via a Met Life–AARP long-term care policy I have been paying into since 1999.

But there are reservations and clauses. For the first three months I have to pay Rusa's salary "out of pocket." Then there will be an "assessment" between the insurance company and the doctors and caregivers and physical therapists to ascertain whether I qualify for more long-term care. To qualify, I must prove that I am unable to perform, without substantial assistance from another individual, at least two "Activities of Daily Living (ADL)" for a period of at least ninety days due to a loss of functional capacity. And there will continue to be more periodic assessments.

Rusa must help me shower, wash my hair, sometimes help me with bathroom hygiene. She does "light housekeeping," though the house has never been this clean. She prepares meals and shops for required items. She drives me to doctors and keeps me from falling. Sometimes when I rise up and try to walk away without my walker, she grabs my shirt from behind and follows me. "We should get me a leash," I tell her.

XIV

I had a speech therapist last summer because the broken neck had caused swelling and I could not pronounce certain consonants. I sounded like someone with a bad cold.

Megan is a life person. Young. Pretty. Smiling, an easy laugher, in her twenties.

From the beginning she knew she wanted to work with children. When she was scarcely out of childhood herself, she took a course in speech therapy for children. At the end she got a graduate degree in speech therapy. There are many kinds of specialists. She chose the specialty of "swallowing."

Perfect teeth. She thinks her face is too round. Many of the exercises require an open mouth. The first time she came I was embarrassed because I hadn't brushed my teeth.

The cat walked back and forth across the table between us. He looked shocked when we did the upscale *ee eze* exercises. And annoyed when we did the hard *k*'s ("Key, Key, Key, Hank, Hank, Hank").

From eight A.M. to two P.M. she works at a facility for brain-damaged people. ("We have lots of young ones. They're the ones who have accidents.")

Megan's mother recently downsized. At first it was an adjustment. She loves it. She moved from a big house to an elegant trailer park. She swims, rides a bike, takes courses. ("She's taking a class on death and dying.")

That started me musing: Are death and dying separate things? Do they live at different addresses?

Death's dwelling seems slightly out of focus. Because what goes on there is always within the lens of someone else's imagination. A child's revenge fantasy or a poet's vision.

The thwarted child who lies in her open coffin: "Oh, now they'll be sorry." Repentant family members: "Oh, why didn't we give her what she wanted while she was still alive?"

(Rebel as a little boy told our grandmother when she thwarted him: "I will not watch your funeral on TV.")

Or one of E. E. Cummings's early poems:

> Buffalo Bill's
> defunct

who used to
ride a watersmooth-silver
    stallion
and break onetwothreefourfivepigeonsjustlikethat

Jesus
he was a handsome man
and what I want to know is
how do you like your blue-eyed boy
Mister Death

The young poet, already employing some of his trademark literary devices, addresses two famous dead people and asks them how they like their "blue-eyed boy," who is Death.

Whereas the thirty-three-year-old Emily Dickinson personifies death as a gentleman picking her up in his carriage:

Because I could not stop for death—
He kindly stopped for me—
The Carriage held but just Ourselves—
And Immortality.

They drive slowly, he knows no haste and she has put away her labor and her leisure for the company of his civility. They pass a school where children are playing and they pass fields of gazing grain and they pass the setting sun. The dews grow quivering and chill because she is wearing gossamer clothes. And they pause before a half-buried house with a scarcely visible roof.

And then centuries go by. They seem shorter than the day when she realized the horses' heads were aiming "toward Eternity."

In the house of dying, specifics of the process are felt and seen and smelled. It has wheelchair ramps and rented hospital beds. The lighting is bright—too bright. There is a no-nonsense, un-lyrical, day-to-day regularity to the goings-on. The medications, the lemon swabs for the mucused mouth, the noisy nebulizer for the lungs, the morphine, the visits from hospice.

XV

Rebel's letter

August 19, 2020

Dear Gail,

Caroline* and I were talking about Monie's† last days when I was in sixth grade.

I don't remember much and was wondering what happened to her that Monie was admitted to Brentwood Rehabilitation Center. I remember that I did not visit regularly as I should have and how much I regret it.

---

* Caroline is Rebel's wife
† Monie was our grandmother, Mother's mother

You are the only person who has these memories so I am hoping you will share them with us.

Love,

Rebel‡

Aug 20, 2020

Dear Rebel,

Monie was "just tired," Mother said.

She was eighty-five-and-a-half. Her spine was disintegrating and when she went to the doctor, he said, "Well, what do you expect at your age?"

She was with Mother at Pinecroft for Christmas 1971. I have a photo of her sitting in the blue chair in the living room. She was still wearing her bathrobe, which may have indicated she was giving up.

Now I think of it, how did she get admitted to Brentwood? She had a private room. Did Mother use her connections? Who paid the bill? I don't know.

I was visiting from Iowa in January during school break and I remember being with her in the private room. I was on the way to the airport and anxious to leave. I kissed her goodbye and I could smell her Dorothy Gray face cream. Soft skin.

Then, as I was exiting the room, there was a mirror placed so I could see her when she could no

---

‡ Rebel, my half brother, twenty-one years younger

longer see me. I still see her expression. Only now I can feel what she felt. It was the expression of someone who knew that family members were getting tired of her. And she accepted that knowledge and was withdrawing into herself.

I tell people that age eighty-six will be enough for me. I have had such a varied, surprising life and I would like NOT to end up in a rehabilitation center watching someone eager to leave my room. But if it happens, at least I know how Monie felt.

Love,

Gail

Monie died two weeks after I visited her. She'd had visitors during the day: Mother, and my (late) half brother Tommy.

A nurse reported: "I was called to her room. She said she couldn't get to sleep, could I give her something. When I returned with the sleeping pill, she gave a startled 'Yip' and passed away, just like that."

XVI

In the night following surgery I had a new experience with reading. I was given oxycodone and was floating on that.

I *partook* of a scene in the *Notebooks of Malte Laurids Brigge*. Malte is Rilke's fictional double. In *The Notebooks* Malte is remembering his grandfather's death. But in my post-surgical waking reverie I experienced the scene as if I were *inside it without words*. I was immersed in it. I was part of the howl in the night.

> *Christoph Detlev's death had been living at Ulsgaard for many, many days now and had spoken to everyone and demanded:* demanded to be carried to the blue room, the little salon, the large hall. And demanded the dogs, and that people should laugh, talk, play, and be quiet, all at the same time. And demanded to see friends, women, people who were dead. He demanded to die.

When night fell at Ulsgaard and the domestics were off duty and tried to go to sleep, his death would roar until the howling dogs were silent and stood on their long, slender, trembling legs. People rose from their beds as if there were a thunderstorm and remained sitting round the lamp until it was over.

This was the wicked, princely death Christoph Detlev had carried within him and nourished in himself his whole life. All excess of pride, will, and lordly vigor that he had not been able to consume in his life had passed into death. The death which now sat, dissipating, at Ulsgaard.

How he would have looked at anyone who suggested that he die any other death than this. He was dying his own hard death.

—*The Notebooks of Malte Laurids Brigge*, translated by M. D. Herter Norton

XVII

W. S. Merwin's short, powerful elegy:
Who would I show it to?

XVIII

During the (what turned out to be) seven months I existed day and night inside the Aspen cervical collar, I could not read a novel. Nor did I watch a movie. It was a *visceral disengagement* that came over me.

After I was home from the surgery and no longer allowed oxycodone, I had a second experience of *partaking* of a novel without reading it. The novel was *The Eye of the Storm*, by Patrick White, the 1973 Nobel winner.

Set in Australia. A dying old woman, Elizabeth Hunter, once stunningly beautiful, still rich, still manipulating those surrounding her (son, daughter, nurses, servants, visitors), relives a violent storm she survived and manages to will her own death when she senses she is no longer in charge. She brings back the storm while sitting on the toilet and evades them all.

It was the wild storm that invaded me and her powerful, selfish life. It felt like I *was* Elizabeth Hunter and I was, as she was, the eye of the storm.

I had read this novel many times, always admiring it, but in 2023 it was no longer on my shelf. I ordered a paperback, but it was so thick I couldn't hold it in bed, so I cut it into three parts and read it piece by piece.

I was smitten with satisfaction and admiration. I appreciated what Patrick White had done. It was so rich and so deep. It had the power to transform a reader.

XIX

I work all day, and get half-drunk at night.
Waking at four to soundless dark, I stare.
In time the curtain-edges will grow light.
Till then I see what's really always there:
Unresting death, a whole day nearer now,
Making all thought impossible but how
And where and when I shall myself die.
Arid interrogation: yet the dread
Of dying, and being dead,
Flashes afresh to hold and horrify.

—First stanza of Philip Larkin's "Aubade"

Philip Larkin began his last great poem, "Aubade," in 1974, when he was fifty-two, and completed it in 1977, after the death of his mother, when he was fifty-five. He died at sixty-three. "Aubade" in French means a song or poem in praise of dawn. Larkin predicted that his poem "would ruin a few Christmas dinners."

The best way to experience the poet's unflinching, horrific five stanzas of imagining "the dread/Of dying, and being dead" is to hear Larkin's voice reading "Aubade" on YouTube. (Be sure to choose the 2009 version.)

I debated whether to start you off with the opening stanza or to pitch you straight into "a special way of being afraid" or "The anaesthetic from which none come round" or "Most things may never happen: this one will."

I chose to start at the beginning.

XX

Sunday, September 18, 2022

Must be up at six tomorrow for the Queen's funeral. What a respite her death has given to me. September 8— September 19. Something large enough to live in for eleven days. Like a book.

> (At her coronation)
> "I will serve you
> for my whole life."

XXI

After finishing *Old Lovegood Girls* I had begun to think of a new set of characters and was searching for the right setting for their peculiar circumstances.

The place must be remote but not inaccessible. Its rarefied air and panoramic vistas would suggest higher reaches for those who dwelled there.

So far there were three girls (eleven, thirteen, and fourteen) and their father and a rich grandfather with his housekeeper and a helicopter pilot who flew him back and forth from his factories.

I remembered the meadow on top of the bald mountain where Pat and I had picnicked and plotted our old age. Then we had descended out of the sunshine, rescued a turtle crossing a country road, and returned to my family's tragedy.

I snatched up my iPad, a device that hadn't existed in October of 1983. I typed the name of the mountain into the Google bar and the screen popped up with Realtors and prices and pictures of what was now called High Meadow Estates.

I called Pat at the Smoky Ridge nursing home:

"What *happened*?"

"Oh, that happened years ago."

"How awful!"

"Think of it this way. At least it is being lived in by humans who enjoy it. *Rich* humans, but still . . . It hasn't had its top sliced off by the strip miners."

XXII

Robert's Twenty-Second Year's Mind

Gail Godwin
to Dan Starer
April 22, 12:15 P.M.

He is very alive. I appreciate him more and more.

Dan Starer
to Gail Godwin
April 22, 2:05 P.M.

I increasingly see him in myself, which is a good thing. I said the Kaddish prayer this morning as I promised him I would. Is there a convenient time/day I could call you? I'd like to catch up.

XXIII

"What I can't get over," said Clare, "is, there we were, up on the mountain on top of the world, planning our old age. And, at about the same time, he was driving across town to make sure he wouldn't have one."

—*A Southern Family* (1987)

October 2, 1983. A bright October day. The day after Mother's birthday, when she liked all her children to come home. I, the oldest, forty-six, who had settled into a writer's life in Woodstock, New York, had flown from Albany. My half sister, Franchelle, thirty, an attorney, had driven up from Columbia, South Carolina, with her husband and two young sons. My half brother Tommy, divorced at twenty-eight, was living at home with his three-year-old son. My half brother Rebel, twenty-five, had driven across state, from Chapel Hill, where he was getting a graduate degree in business.

Pat was taking me to a new place. After her adventures and transformations, she had returned via Iceland,

Austin, and New York City to teach in her home state at Mars Hill College. Each time I came home it was a point of pride for Pat to introduce me to some new place we had never known as children.

We had to park at the bottom of the mountain and pass the entrance test of footing it over intimidating rocks and small chasms of ruts.

"There's hardly a road here," I said, out of breath already. "Nobody's been here in years."

"He's a retired navy officer. He comes in by helicopter. The word is that hikers are welcome to picnic as long as they clean after themselves."

"How did you know about it?"

"Someone tells someone and someone tells someone else. It's not in any hiking-trails guide. Jim brought me here once. We were still hiking together though we no longer slept together."

With frequent stops, mostly for me, we climbed up, up through rugged landscape interspersed with stands of trees already shedding their colorful leaves. We looked down a hill where someone had given up on a Christmas tree farm. I was wondering how much longer I could hold out before admitting I couldn't go a step farther when Pat said, "Let's catch our breaths before the final sprint."

After that, the air grew lighter and we traipsed through high grasses into a meadow bright with sunshine. All around us were vistas of mountains fading into the horizon.

"What is this?" I said.

"It's called High Meadow. It's one of the grassy balds."

"Balds?"

"They're still an ecological mystery. Nobody knows for certain how they came to be. They're mostly on ridge tops in the southern Appalachians. There's some mentions in Cherokee legends."

"Isn't there some music called 'A Night on Bald Mountain'?"

"Mussorgsky. His Bald Mountain was in Russia. But no orchestra would play it . . ."

"Oh, I *hate* stories like that!"

"Later Rimsky-Korsakov made another version, which is famous. It was in that Walt Disney *Fantasia* movie."

"I saw that movie but all I remember is my mother was enchanted by it and I thought it was boring."

"I saw it, too, but don't remember even that."

We threw ourselves down in the meadow and lay looking up at the sky. Ranges of mountains encircled us. A hawk spiraled closer and closer until we could see its face. It was noontime.

Our topic today was: How were we going to hold on to our power in old age? Death wasn't interesting to us yet. We were forty-six.

Three years later, Sherry Arden, an editor at Morrow, reading the galleys of *A Southern Family*, remarked, "That 'Olympians' chapter of two women on top of the mountain—that chapter alone is worth the price of the book."

At the end of the chapter, when Julia and Clare are driving Clare back to her family, they see a turtle starting to cross the country road. Julia pulls off the road and they run to rescue the turtle, which, surprisingly fast, had completed half its journey across the asphalt.

As we came close, it withdrew into its shell. I picked it up—it was heavy—and balanced it evenly in my palms. It had a handsome shell with orange spots. We escorted it to the other side and set it down in the tall grasses, arranging it so it faced forward into the woods ahead.

This was not a heavily traveled road. The turtle and its ancestors must have crossed at this spot for generations with only the rare casualty. This turtle would probably have made it on its own today. But we were elated.

Returning to the car, I said something like, "One more tragedy averted."

"Yes," said Pat. "It's a good omen."

All the family cars were gone when we pulled up at the house. The door was not only unlocked but open.

"This is not normal," I said. "They keep this place locked up like a fortress."

"Do you want me to stay for a while?" asked Pat.

"No, I'm just acting like a child. It's just that it's never happened before, that I came home and there was nobody *there.* God, I loved that place you took me today. So high up and the sun on the meadow and the hawk. Just you and me, on top of the world."

"Olympians on Olympus," said Pat.

XXIV

April 27, 2023
_____

Today is Sister Winter's birthday. She was born in County Galway, Ireland, in 1913, the year after my mother was born in Selma, Alabama. They both were named Kathleen. Late in life, in their seventies, they started a friendship. She was my eighth-grade teacher at St. Genevieve's and we stayed close until her death, at eighty-eight, on Good Friday in 2001, a week and two days before Robert's death, at seventy-seven, on Sunday, April 22, 2001.

She was "Mother Winters," age thirty-eight, when I walked into her classroom. After the Vatican II changes, she became "Sister Winters" and stopped wearing her habit.

She has been a star player in my dream repertory of significant figures, right up there with Mother; Robert; Monie; my stepfather, Frank; and Pat. She has remained a powerful and necessary influence throughout my lifetime. I changed my handwriting to look like hers. In 1951 she was my wise model when I was desperate for one. She became my spiritual mother and my mentor.

The first Mentor was an intimate friend of Odysseus, and when Odysseus embarked on his odyssey he left Mentor as the adviser to his son, Telemachus. Greek mythology tells us that Mentor was Athena in disguise. The symbology enriches my picture of what Sister Winters embodies for me.

She was a storyteller whose tales were rich with humor and connections. About becoming a nun, she told us that her family in Ireland raised horses, and when she was about twelve her father brought home a new mare. They hadn't realized she was pregnant, and she gave birth to a scrawny little creature who looked like a baby goat huddling in the shadows. The mother would have nothing to do with her, so the family raised her. They named her Shadow, and she grew up with the dogs and the children. She was allowed inside the house, where she would put her head in your lap and drool on your book. Then one day she "jumped" one of the children in play and they realized it was time to send Shadow off to a trainer who would teach her how to be a horse.

Kathleen Winters left home at nineteen to join an order of nuns in Belgium, and after she was professed they allowed her to tell her family goodbye before they sent her to America. When her father came to meet her at the station he was embarrassed and didn't know how to act toward this woman in a habit.

"And I felt awkward myself until it came to me like an inspiration. 'Well, Father,' I said, 'you see they've made a nun out of me just like they made a horse out of Shadow.' And he laughed and we hugged and it was fine after that. When we got home the rest of them were a little awkward at first, but he repeated what I'd said at the train station and it was all fine after that" (*A Southern Family*, pp. 536–37, "Anniversary").

When Mother and Sister Winters found themselves back in Asheville in their seventies, they frequently went out to lunch and on outings. Both were interested in what was happening in the world and both were ardent about the spiritual life. Mother was a high Episcopalian and Sister Winters was a Roman Catholic.

"I just cannot get used to having women serve as priests," Mother told her friend. "After all, Jesus was a man."

"Well, Kathleen, he couldn't very well have come back as both," Sister Winters said.

So much of the "Anniversary" chapter has been delightful for me to read almost thirty-six years later. I had captured some of the essence of Sister Winters through the character of Sister Patrick and some of the spirit of my mother, Kathleen, in the character of Lily Quick.

It was like acknowledging a gift from myself. But, alas, there is so much more to both Kathleens!

XXV

When the editor at Morrow was reading the galleys of *A Southern Family* in 1986 and remarked that "Olympians," the second chapter, about the two women on top of the mountain, was "by itself worth the price of the book," I was still fresh from writing it and knew what she meant.

But looking back so many years later, I had to read that chapter to remember what was in it.

When Julia and I talk of becoming old, thinks Clare, we always agree that one has to take a position on it, that one has to *prepare an image of oneself* that one can grow into.

Today on the bald mountain Julia says, "I look forward to reaching the age when I don't care what people think, when I will say what I damn please and live how I like."

They agree they need a power base to do that from, to be the kind of witch who is feared or admired—perhaps even loved—rather than shunned or burned at the stake.

There is the power base of money. Clare tells of her visit to a rich old widowed aunt in her eighties who lives in a hotel suite in Birmingham. The aunt welcomes her in a queenly brocaded dressing gown and asks if she is hungry after her train ride. Clare has visions of a sumptuous room service trolley, but instead of picking up the phone, the old aunt asks her to open a can of vegetable beef soup and cooks it on the coils of her stove burner. "Isn't this fun," cries the aunt as they eat the lukewarm soup out of rare china soup bowls, "just you and me all on our own without anyone lurking around *waiting* on us."

"And she looked so happy, with all her millions, to be eating her own home-cooked glop in her hotel suite, that I delighted in her, whereas if she had been poor I would have felt pity."

Julia speaks of the power base of fame. And they cite examples: Georgia O'Keeffe and Dame Rebecca West at ninety "lunging" at her interviewer "like a shaggy old lioness in a too-tight pearl leash."

And you can be one of those, Julia says generously, no matter how old you get or what you look like, because of the work you've done.

Then she adds that she herself will have to rely on something else because she's not known to the public. ("I'm too vain to tolerate becoming invisible . . . Until very recently I was used to walking down a street or into a room and having people snap to attention . . . I want to be seen as myself, whatever age I am.")

"But wait," counters Clare, "they weren't seeing you as yourself in your 'glorious years,' youth, either. They were seeing you as a 'pretty young girl,' just as people snap to attention at the sight of a really pretty tulip in this year's garden . . . [I] would have to be a lot more famous than I am for even one stranger aboard an airplane to connect my face with my books. [People] see me as just a woman, then just an older woman, then just an old woman."

No, here's an exception. "I was flying back to New York after my book tour last spring, feeling oh so conspicuously notorious after all my interviews, and I sat next to a man who asked me if I was a nun . . . I was wearing black slacks, a black turtleneck sweater, and a nondescript blue blazer. Also a little pendant on a gold chain; it's just a bunch of gold grapes with a pearl in the middle, but it could be mistaken for a cross . . . And I was reading *Framley Parsonage*, which he might have thought was a religious book. And I hadn't spoken until he started the conversation, and I didn't volunteer any information about myself."

"Did you, afterwards?"

"Oh, yes. Our plane was delayed in Pittsburgh and we had dinner together. And I could see him slowly become attracted to me. We had a very good talk. He turned out to be a serious man who had thought a lot about the proper way to fulfill his responsibilities. For instance, he told me he had been brought up an atheist, but when he had children he decided they should at least know about some formal religion, and after he researched them all and concluded that the Dutch Reformed Church was the most sensible, the whole family joined the Dutch Reformed Church. And he was very unhappy that his daughter had just divorced: he said he couldn't help thinking he had failed her in some way. That was the kind of man he was. And after we landed at LaGuardia, and he had already said goodbye and had gone off, and I was calling Felix from a pay phone, he came all the way back from the taxi rank to tell me that he just wanted me to know that he couldn't imagine a better person than me to take around the world with him on his boat . . . His wife's some sort of invalid; he didn't specify, but . . . he did say she was going to be so pleased when he brought her my book and told her he had met the author on the plane. But the point is, I think he finally was attracted to something in me that had nothing to do with how I looked or how old I was, or even the fact I had written and published several books. [It] made me feel good for days afterwards: if a stranger who started off thinking I was a nun could come around in two or three hours to seeing me as the ideal companion for a round-the-world boat trip, then there's hope, don't you see? Only, we'll have to rely more on our *essences*, whatever they are, than on sticking up like the showiest tulips of the season and making a smashing first impression."

"So maybe your man wasn't so far wrong when he mistook your occupation," said Julia. "There is always, I suppose, the power base of a secret, inviolate spiritual life."

And Clare thinks of another power base: that of knowing yourself a beloved local person. She thinks she's already got a good start—Julia's students drop by her house; her friends are devoted, leave little gifts for her when she's out, put steaks in her refrigerator. But Clare is afraid to tell her this, because Julia's still touchy about having come home. She's afraid it might signify she's given up, that she's used Duty as an excuse to abandon the struggle for Self. Why doesn't she expand her dissertation into a book?

She says it was about an aspect of slavery nobody's gone into yet. But if she doesn't hurry up, someone is going to beat her to it. The trouble with her is, it *wouldn't* kill her as it would me. I can just hear her saying, "Actually, I'm glad X published that book on how Black slave culture influenced the slaveholders and enriched the culture of the South. I couldn't have done it any better."

The arc of Pat's life has supplied me with more than material for a novel; it has illustrated to me that there are moral natures *outside* of books that are superior to mine.

Getting to Know Death is my tenth book edited by Nancy Miller, who has consistently stretched my mind with such questions as the one below.

She writes, "What makes her moral nature better? That she's not driven to be ambitious?"

I had to think about this. What about my drive to be ambitious? Haven't I always thought of it as a character flaw? Well . . .

My grandmother Monie used to tell me, "The thing about you, you want to be everyone and excel in everybody's talents."

And on a chill November walk with Sister Winters, when she was in her late seventies and I in my early fifties, I suddenly challenged her:

"What makes you so sure that God loves you?"

"Well, Gail, you have to love yourself first," she replied.

Am I finally able to love myself at the age of eighty-six if I admit that I seem to have been wired to be determined to excel?

Yes, I think I can.

XXVI

"When you're a young writer, you subtract the birth dates of authors from their publication dates and feel panic or hope. When you're an old writer, you observe the death dates of your favorite writers and you reflect on their works and their lives."

So began my essay in the *New York Times Book Review* (December 10, 2010). I had titled it "The Old Writer," but the editors changed it to "Working on the Ending."

The drawing illustrating the piece was of a scythe pursuing a ragged line across the page to catch up with a pen. Above the ragged line was handwritten, "I'm not finished . . ."

I had just turned eighteen when publication panic first struck. Nineteen-year-old Françoise Sagan's *Bonjour Tristesse* had just been published in English. My panic was also laced with grudging jealousy because it was the story of a seventeen-year-old girl's time at the beach with her father, who had been absent from her childhood. I was at the beach, getting to know a father who had been absent from my childhood.

And now this French girl had become internationally famous when I hadn't achieved anything, AND she had hijacked my material.

"This past year I outlived Henry James, who died two months short of his 73rd birthday." Thus begins the second paragraph of my old-writer essay.

As of today, May 4, 2023, I have outlived George Eliot (age sixty-one), Elizabeth Bowen (age seventy-three), Leo Tolstoy (age eighty-two), and, finally, Samuel Beckett (age eighty-three).

The missing favorite is Jane Austen. She died at age forty-one, decades before the age when I started observing death dates. Causes are still being considered: Addison's disease (acute adrenal failure), cancer, lupus, lymphoma, and the latest, arsenic, which was present in many medications.

A year and a half after her partner George Henry Lewes's death, in 1878, Eliot married the twenty-years-younger John Cross. On their Venice honeymoon he jumped out of the window into the Grand Canal. The gesture may have been knee-jerk panic at what Rebecca Mead surmises could have been "a gross inequity of desire." Eliot died eleven months later from kidney failure.

Elizabeth Bowen died of lung cancer after various respiratory illnesses.

In the middle of the night of October 28, 1910, Count Leo Tolstoy left home in secret to get away from his wife's nagging. He died of pneumonia at the home of the stationmaster of Astapovo, a small railway station.

His dying turned into a media event. Not only was he a world-famous writer but authorities feared his reputation as a pacifist and supporter of peasants might start a revolution. His last words were to his daughter Tatyana: "Well, this is the end, that is all." By the time his wife, Sophia, arrived, he did not recognize her.

XXVII

The Dying of Henry James

"So it has come at last. The distinguished thing."

Henry James has been often misreported saying this just before he expired, and for a while I accepted the misreports. It sounded just like him, but these were not his words just before he expired.

Take care to fact-check websites with titles like "Last Words of Famous People."

Earlier on the day of his stroke, the writer wrote to his niece Peggy. He recounted his recent illnesses, complained of sleepless nights, and peevishly questioned why a certain writer "should be lionized at this time" when his work belonged to "such an antediluvian past." Then he felt tired and ended his letter with the words "The pen drops from my hand."

Next morning the maid found him lying on the floor, his left leg having given way under him. She and his long-term valet got him to bed. By the time his secretary, Miss Bosanquet, arrived, he told her he had had a stroke "in the most approved fashion." He told other friends that his first thought as he fell was "So it has come at last—the distinguished thing." Another friend later reported she heard James say, "It's the beast in the jungle, and it's sprung."

On the following day James had a second stroke, paralyzing his left side.

Twenty-four hours later, James rallied and called for a thesaurus to find the exact word for his condition. "Paralytic" didn't sound right.

Two diaries, one by his sister-in-law Alice James and one by his secretary Miss Bosanquet, reported the details of his mental wanderings. He asked where he was, where certain manuscripts were.

When Mrs. James brushed his hair, he told her, "Ardent brushing does not mitigate my troubles."

He thought he was Napoleon Bonaparte and proposed new decorations to the Louvre and the Tuileries.

In late December of 1915 some movement returned to James's arm and leg.

In January he mentally made the journey back to Lamb House in Rye.

He imagined one of his plays was being produced and asked Mrs. James, "What effect will my madness have on the house?"

Certain blessed writers get a biographer worthy of them. James was a blessed writer. Leon Edel took almost twenty years to complete his five-volume biography of Henry James. Worthy biographers interlace their subject's life with the art produced by their subjects.

Here is Leon Edel's interlacing comment about the dying of Henry James:

> These partial records of Henry James's mental confusion suggest a kind of heroic struggle to regain his grasp on reality in the midst of his death-in-life. Taken together they suggest that in some mysterious way the master may have been living out that "terror of consciousness" with which he had sought to endow his hero in *The Sense of the Past*, the unfinished novel he had been trying to complete.
>
> On the evening before his stroke James had turned over some of the pages of his novel-in-progress. James, in his notes for *The Sense of the Past*, has his hero waking to the year 1820 with his knowledge of the future, feeling "in danger of passing for a madman."

His sister-in-law Alice James wrote:

> He seems like a tired child . . . enjoying his food and the sitting on a big lounge in the window whence he can look out at the river . . . He thinks he is

> voyaging . . . and sometimes he asks for his glasses and paper and imagines that he writes. And sometimes his hand moves over the counterpane as if writing.

His last words were spoken to his sister-in-law. "Stay with me, Alice, stay with me." He lapsed into unconsciousness. He did try to speak at six P.M. on the day before he died, but his words were unintelligible. On February 28, 1916, he could take no nourishment. He sighed three times at long intervals.

Alice wrote, "He was gone. Not a shadow on his face nor the contraction of a muscle."

Some years before his death, Henry James wrote an essay, "Is There Life After Death?" His answer: physical life—none. What lived beyond life was what the creative consciousness had found and made: and only if enshrined in enduring form.

And in one of the final sentences of the essay: "I reach beyond the laboratory brain."

XXVIII

Before I reached the age of eighty-two, I could say "I have outlived everyone but Tolstoy, Beckett, and my grandmother." After that I amended it to "everyone but Beckett and my grandmother." Then it was just "my grandmother."

She died a full six months before her eighty-sixth birthday. I will reach my eighty-sixth birthday in the middle of next month.

I became motivated by Beckett's work in my thirties, when I was studying for my Ph.D. at the University of Iowa. A professor on my doctoral committee gave me a mimeographed copy of "Imagination Dead Imagine." Beckett wrote the story in French, then translated it to English.

I read it again and again. Today you can google the piece and choose to listen to recordings from a variety of narrators. I think it would come across better if you hear it first. You can also hear it set to music. (Try the Michael Roth version for voices and string quartet on YouTube.)

But simply reading it from that purple mimeograph page in Iowa made me rabid. To try something like that. And I did.

This morning I told Rusa I needed to go upstairs and find something in my study.

"Going upstairs" these days, I hold tight to my cane in my right hand and grab the banister with my left hand. Arik, the physical therapist from Archcare, showed me how to do it. Your left foot steps to the first step at the same time you are pushing up with your cane in the right hand. ("Stay close to the rail, Gail.") Then you bring your right leg up to stand next to the left. And breathe. "Go one step at a time like that until you're at the top. You are in no hurry. Why are you in such a rush all the time?"

Then make a turn to the right without twisting your neck, enter your study, followed closely by Rusa, who's holding your T-shirt from behind.

Another right to face the bookshelves against the wall. The literary quarterlies are stacked on the bottom shelf. It's not in the front row of any stack. Remove all the front row, Rusa holding the books, and scan the row in back. Oh, please, be there. There it is. Its spine says: *James Joyce Quarterly*, Summer 1971.

Success. Now repeat the stairs thing going down, right hand on banister, cane in left hand. Both feet on the same step. Breathe. Then down a step. Breathe, then repeat.

Until you're in your bed again, opening the *James Joyce Quarterly*. The Summer 1971 issue was "The Beckett Issue."

Inside is my three-and-a-half-page contribution.

"A critification of Beckett's 'residua' by the gifted young novelist Gail Godwin"—that's how the guest editor describes it.

For Samuel Beckett: More

Go over it again. Fill in the spaces. Draw out the implications. Reassess the value of the experience. Weigh the burden of the loss. Explore and adumbrate. Repeat without fear. The sun is hot and accelerates our end. No matter. Till that comes more.

He could contain all of me though in those days I grew fast. He was a man of infinite capacities though he never left his chair. One day I climbed aboard and found it promising. I settled myself in the angle most mutually comfortable and there I remained. I was a willing passenger to the end. I was never bored. He always gave a little more than I could take and he never repeated himself.

Those are the first two paragraphs. Reading the "critification of Beckett's 'residua'" fifty-two years later, I think: "Good job!" to that thirty-four-year-old graduate student. You did it, you got into his rhythms and told your own tale in an essential way. Help me to do this again.

Shortly before he died, Robert said about his work:
I used to try to be original.
Now I try to be clear and essential.

> —Help me try to do this again, I say to the thirty-four-year-old writer of "More."
> —What is "this"? Be more specific, she says.
> —Well, to fill in some background, I need to ramble a little.
> —Okay. But keep it short.

During the three years I was working on my fourteenth novel, *Flora*, my writing style was undergoing change. I was shaping a shorter, sharper sentence and heading toward an essential focus in theme, almost severe at times. Was I becoming impatient with excess or just losing more words?

Sometimes the thesaurus obliged with the word, a word I wanted. When it refused, I would ask myself, "Do you really *need* this word?" If the word was an adjective or adverb, I often found I could do without it or I would tell myself, "You can come back to this later. Leave a blank for now."

My working notes for *Flora* contain pep talks and guides toward what I didn't know yet.

> *Constructing this lean tale about the underpinnings of the self may lead into unexplored territory.*

> *A young girl, isolated and threatened in some way. What measures would she take to protect herself and what would the fallout be?*

The thirty-four-year-old graduate student stops me.

—Okay, the rambling notes helped you at the time, but let's get back to the topic.

—What was the topic?

—How you can go on *now*. What did your thirty-four-year-old self absorb from that first exposure to Beckett, and what can you learn from him that will fire you up *now*? Now that you've read all his books and seen *Waiting for Godot* twice, and read James Knowlson's *Damned to Fame: The Life of Samuel Beckett*, what unexplored territory does his example point you toward now?

—Well, I ask myself, How much can I strip away and *essentially* tell my story the way you did with

"More," when all you had read was "Imagination Dead Imagine"?

—That's a good start. Just remember that it's your own tale, with the excess stripped away. You're not competing with Beckett. You're just motivated by what he risked!

XXIX

I realized that Joyce had gone as far as one could
in the direction of knowing more, [being] in control
of one's material. He was always adding to it; you
only have to look at his proofs to see that. I
realized that my own way was impoverishment
in lack of knowledge and in taking away, in
subtracting rather than adding.

—SAMUEL BECKETT, TO HIS BIOGRAPHER JAMES KNOWLSON

James Knowlson organized an exhibition to honor Beckett's work after he had been awarded the Nobel Prize in
1969. Knowlson, a professor at the University of Reading,
England, also founded the Beckett Archive at Reading.
In 1972, an American publisher asked Knowlson to write
Beckett's biography, but Knowlson declined when Beckett
indicated that he hoped it would be his work rather than
his life that was placed under the microscope. "So,"
Knowlson writes in his preface to the biography, "over
the next two decades, fascinated by his writing and

particularly his stage and television plays, I went on to write about that work, corresponding with him regularly and meeting him many times each year."

Meanwhile, a first biography was written by Deirdre Bair and published in 1978.

Again approached by a publisher asking him to write a Beckett biography, Knowlson wrote to Beckett that he would not proceed without an unambiguous yes from him. Beckett replied with a one-line note.

To biography of me by you it's Yes.

When they next met, Beckett told Knowlson that he would cooperate fully with him so that the authorized biography would be by someone who knew his work well.

Knowlson could not agree with Beckett that his life was absolutely separated from his work. Knowlson cited many examples of Beckett's images of his childhood in Ireland. A man and a boy walking hand in hand over the mountains . . . a larch tree turning green a week before the others, the sounds of stonecutters on the hills above his home.

Oh, yes said Beckett. Those images were obsessional. And he went on to cite many more.

But Knowlson says between his life and his work there is a vast difference in the way these experiences are used and transformed in Beckett's early work and his post–World War II writing. "In the later period he does indeed escape from any direct depiction of life by writing himself out of the text, by making the text self-referential or even virtually self-generating. The life material remains but is simply located at several removes below the surface [. . .] Beckett's late work seeks to explore the nature of being and is consequently less concerned with the superficial and transitory."

Certain blessed writers get a biographer worthy of them. Worthy biographers interlace their subject's life with the art produced by their subject.

An exciting experiment for an Old Writer:

How much of your story can you convey with the excess stripped away?

XXX

The writer John Bowers told me of a writing teacher who trained her students by having them copy the writing of famous writers. This was after World War II, when creative writing workshops first came into being. This particular workshop was in Chicago, I think. Such a scene! A class filled with GIs on the GI Bill pounding away on typewriters, copying Hemingway, Faulkner, Sinclair Lewis, Conrad. Could such an exercise help you become a writer? John said yes. "It got you into a rhythm."

I have decided to copy out in handwriting the rest of "More." Maybe I'll slip into the rhythm I seek: the rhythm of a story boiled down to essentials.

I left off at the end of the second paragraph of "More":

"He always gave a little more than I could take and he never repeated himself."

I think people worried about my welfare with him. They were afraid he would corrupt me. But his corruption was all the welfare I needed. Other children played jacks and hide-and-seek and went home to supper. His lap was my home.

I played with his penis which was capable of endless surprises. He rocked me to sleep against his shoulder with the reverberations of his strange spare stories. Often we dozed together in our inhalations and our exhalations. His left temple pressed upon my crown. Sometimes we dreamed the same dream. I should make it clear we never repeated a dream. His rule was never repeat anything. One of a kind only. He dreamed his part of the dream and I dreamed mine. Once I dreamed I was killing him and he woke dying and we wept into each other's eyes. We were happy together. He had to tell the stories I had to hear. Just those and no more. He never repeated himself and he never told a story superfluous to our needs. I snuggled in the lonely space between his trunk and thighs and his voice filled the greedy hollow of my ear. As soon as my body grew to accommodate him I filled other voids. He too.

He hit me once. It was when I looked out of the window. I saw it was a fine day and I asked if we could leave the chair and go out for a walk. It was then I learned of his restriction. He shouted it at me only once and hit me once across the mouth. I had nothing to stop the blood. He licked it away himself and slipped inside of me. He told the most perfect story yet about the two of us going for a walk.

So we went on together in our chair. Nothing ever repeated. No limit to what we could do in one chair. Stories and filling the other's voids. Rocking and filling our own.

Let me tell you about the stories. I can't repeat them because I only heard each once. But I will try to convey their shape and we can build on that. Contrary to what you might think his stories were limited. A limitless man telling deliberately limited stories. He cut them to essentials. Honed them down to the bone. There would be time enough for flesh later he said. He couldn't be bothered with that. No time for adjectives or proper names. Prune all distracting appendages. Yet he made me ravenous by his constant holding back. With the flat of his language he arrested the growth of miracles but not until you'd felt their sting. Turning and turning upon the point of the pain. Probing the limits of the void. Leave the extenuations to others. I sat almost continuously, my legs wrapped around his trunk. My ankles hooked behind his broad back. Our fore-heads pressed together. But infinite variation in the pattern of the rocking. Constant innovation in the finger tracings on the other's back. Never a repetition. Most of the time we kept our eyes closed while we joined at the probing point.

Once I asked him about his restriction. That was permitted. I could ask anything once and he would answer it. Contrary to what I had believed he was not crippled though now his legs were possibly useless. He said one day he simply sat down in the chair. I climbed up shortly after. Though he doubted whether my coming made any difference. He would have gone on telling the stories even to the bare walls. One void was as good as another. His remark wounded. I said other voids can't do what I am doing now. It's all the same in the end he said. Though his stern face was suffused with delight. Such contradictions kept me in the chair.

It might have gone on like this interminably if I had not looked out the window again. I say again but I did not repeat myself. The first time I had looked out with my left eye. This time his eyes were closed. We were between stories. Wrapped in our mutual silence and probing the void. My left cheek pressed against his left cheek. My right eye free to wander. It wandered out the window. It was a fine day. Fields filled with flowers all repeating themselves endlessly. Same sky. Then I saw you coming along in the field one step much like the other and possibly the same. I wanted to go out for a walk but could not say it aloud again. I felt his left eye flicker questioningly against my blasphemous thought. We were so close you see. I closed the guilty eye at once and snuggled by mistake into a position we had already used up. With a cry of disgust he ejected me from the chair. I lay cold and empty on the floor at his feet. I did make one serious attempt to scale his legs a second time being careful not to repeat the movements of my former climb. But as my head crested the shield of his knee one enraged blue eye locked with mine and Goodbye he said. He never repeated himself.

I crawled out into the coveted sun which now burns me quicker towards death and you found me there. How strange I must have seemed to you. How pale and otherworldly this creature like yourself yet unlike struggling to the harsh light. You were alone in your fields not expecting anybody. You were generous by nature. You covered me with flowers until my skin grew hardened to sun. I taught you how to kiss.

Your kisses were all alike but had on the whole a calming action. For long monotonous stretches of afternoon you massaged my useless legs till I could limp along beside you. We became companion-lovers in that field of flowers. Then one day I grew strong and less grateful and began to desire his intricate novelties again. I took you by the hand and drew you in till you desired them too. I corrupted you.

Now we pace the limits of our field like caged animals your ear bent obsessively to me as I tell you how he plundered me first leaving a hollow that no one else can fill and how no walk we take no matter how long or where we walk will measure up to his story of the walk which distilled all walks down to their essential desirability. Sometimes you weep and I lick away your tears. But it's just a variation of the time he licked away my blood. Anything we do now is an extenuation of the things he would only let us do once. Our future must be repetitions of his single themes. Yet I have found with you an unexpected consolation. Mutual suffering was a thing I never had with him. So we've outdistanced him there. Though he would call it flesh upon the bones of his essentials. No matter. It trails behind it the progeny of hope. That hitherto unarticulated vulgarity.

We'll go on collaborating. You and I. Refining and emending and enveloping and reiterating our one story. And sometimes decorating like the time you covered me in flowers. It's all we have and so we'll go on. Our brave legs scissoring through the flowers. I'll tell it to you again and again each time adding something new. The things you don't know will keep me going. Though I'm like him. The audience makes no difference to the telling. One void is as good as another. If you weren't here I'd tell it to the flowers.

Go over it again. Fill in the spaces. Draw out the implications. Reassess the value of the experience. Weigh the burden of the loss. Explore and adumbrate. Repeat without fear. The sun is hot and accelerates our end. No matter. Till that comes more.

XXXI

Soon it will be one year since I went out to water the little dogwood and fell on the gravel and broke my neck. Twelve days after that I will celebrate my eighty-sixth birthday.

Already I have outlived everybody on my list. My grandmother died six months before her eighty-sixth birthday. So I have outlived Monie.

Last Saturday Jane Toby came and carried away the second part of *Getting to Know Death: A Meditation.* She brought an almond cake laced with rhubarb.

After Robert died I decided to get someone to transcribe my apprentice-year journals, three file cabinet drawers full of notebooks covering the years 1961–1969, the years when I was working on becoming a writer. First I had to go through each notebook and cross out the over-the-top indiscretions and promiscuities, leaving a blue-penciled wake of x'ed-out notebook entries. Then

I had to find a discreet typist who might well glance through the notebooks' x'ed-out parts as well.

Someone suggested I try a friend of Theodore Sturgeon's widow and that's how I found Jane, who transcribed the bowdlerized years of 1961–1969, which were published as *The Making of a Writer*, volumes one and two, edited with commentary by Rob Neufeld.

And here Jane was, a year younger than I, still living, driving, typing, baking her pies and cakes and writing poetry and tutoring students in the Italian language. And now she has transcribed the first part of *Getting to Know Death* and on Saturday drove away with most of the rest of it.

Rusa brought us tea and slices of the delicious almond-rhubarb cake and Jane told me of going to New Jersey for a reunion with the class of Nigerian boys she taught in her Peace Corps years. They live here now and have raised children and excelled in their many professions. One is a spine surgeon.

Jane was and is a petite person. She cuts her own white hair. I asked her if I could include my favorite of her recent poems:

Transformations

The milkweed flies
from its pod,
its house of brown

Cold rises
out of the center
of the earth

There is a harshness
that grows more intense
as you walk deeper

into the field.
You begin to believe
in the cold

in the blackbirds
lifting the last limbs of light
from the trees

The colored leaves
are gone
You walk into a world

that is alien
and you bless it.
You bless unrelenting change.

XXXII

The war years as a whole had a profound effect on Beckett [. . .] It was one thing to appreciate fear, danger, anxiety, and deprivation intellectually. It was quite another to live them himself, as he had done at the time he was stabbed or when he was in hiding or on the run [. . .] Beckett's later prose and plays arise directly from his experiences of radical uncertainty, disorientation, exile, hunger, and need. [. . .] Humor had proved, however, a strong lifeline many times before. And in occupied Paris, in Roussillon, and his St-Lo, it became [. . .] one of the few things that made life at all tolerable.

—James Knowlson, *Damned to Fame: The Life of Samuel Beckett* (Simon & Schuster, 1996), p. 318

XXXIII

Logan Roy is dead, having keeled over in the toilet of a private jet [. . .] It was an event that any "Succession" fan knew would probably happen sometime— Logan's first brush with death, a stroke, came in the series pilot—just maybe not, paradoxically, so soon. (Sunday's episode was only the third of 10 this season.)

[. . .] Brian Cox, who for three-plus seasons played Logan with a leonine ferocity, seemed as surprised as anyone to learn that his character was fated for such a swift demise.

"He [Jesse Armstrong, the show's creator] called me, and he said, "Logan's going to die," Cox said. "And I thought, 'Oh, that's fine.' I thought he would die in about Episode 7 or 8, but Episode 3, I thought . . .'*Well that's a bit early.*'"

—Austin Considine, "How Brian Cox Felt about That Big Episode 3 Twist in *Succession*, *The New York Times*, April 9, 2023

XXXIV

Sometimes a truth is buried
under what seemed at the time
the most interesting story.

Now I have outlived everybody on my list. The last ones were Beckett and my grandmother. Then it was just my grandmother, whose fifty-first year's mind is January 21, 2023.

In the wee hours of that new day in 1972, she rang for the nurse. She couldn't get to sleep. "Would you bring me something?" When the nurse returned with the sleeping pill, Monie gave a surprised little "yip," and was gone.

The thing none of us living will ever know was why she was called Monie. I remember being asked by a classmate when we were about ten. "Because she had all the money," I told the classmate. Which was a preposterous invention. Monie's income was from her late husband's benefits from the Southern Railway, for which he worked as a master mechanic. (The other benefit was her lifelong travel pass on the railroad.) My mother's jobs as a teacher and newspaper reporter were what sustained us.

When I was edging into old age myself and was the keynote speaker at Kanuga Conference Center in Hendersonville, North Carolina, Father Gale Webbe, the Episcopal priest of my childhood, in his upper nineties by then, was introducing me to the audience. He recounted those earlier years of mine and spoke of my "formidable grandmother." Formidable! Did she really come across to him as formidable? When I heard him say this, I thought, No, she was *shy*.

Yes, but there was more: Proud, distant, diffident, wary, introverted, undemonstrative, controlled, self-restrained?

Not one of them catches her. All of them could apply to the person who raised me, the Monie I knew.

But she wasn't "just" any one of them.

How about a combination? The self-restrained power in our lives? The restraining power? The warily controlling power?

I have derived two strong characters, quite different people, from my experience of Monie: Edith Dewar Barnstorff, in *The Odd Woman* (1974), and Honora Drake Anstruther, in *Flora* (2013). In each of those novels I caught large swaths of her, but in both novels I buried something essential that haunts me now.

In my dreams she resides in the apartment where we left her when, in the late spring of 1948, my mother secretly married Frank and took me away to live with them at 1000 Sunset Drive, an apartment in a big house on top of a mountain. I was eleven.

The breakup, in early evening, brought out the worst in all of us. My mother was torn, a fence-sitter. Frank yelled and accused, Monie wept and threatened to call a powerful cousin of hers, Frank yelled and mocked her. I don't remember doing anything but watching to see what would happen.

And then we left 286 Charlotte Street for 1000 Sunset Drive. A polio scare kept us from any meeting all summer.

In my dreams, Monie is still living in our ground-floor apartment on Charlotte Street. And I am trying to get to her. The dream landscape has altered—new buildings, houses, streets. But the ground-floor apartment, sometimes just the apartment, floating all alone in the altered landscape, is still there, containing my grandmother.

Sometimes I make it back and am reunited with her. Sometimes everything is gone.

As I was writing about all the ones I have outlived, I knew she waited at the end of the line. As of today, May 20, it is twenty-nine days until my eighty-sixth birthday.

And it was not until now that I realized she was a big mystery in my life, she contained more than I ever thought to imagine about her.

So how to begin to uncover what I never wanted to know until now?

Toward the end of *Flora*, we read one of "Nonie's" letters to a troubled young woman (Flora) seeking advice.

Starting with the adage "Spoken word is slave; unspoken is master," Honora Anstrather continues,

> Just keep in mind that people do not read minds. They judge by what they see and hear, and you are a well-favored young woman with a modest, unaffected voice. Just let those two things work for you. You will be surprised how far they'll carry you. Hold yourself like someone who sets value on her person and remember that a simple, courteous response will get you through practically anything. You don't need to be witty (some people just aren't gifted that way) or tell private things about yourself or your family.
>
> You warm this old heart the way you lavish praise on me, but I am basically just a country girl without much education who has tried to keep her dignity and make the most of the cards dealt her.

Edna Rogers Krahenbuhl (1886–1972) could have written those words. I possess the torn-off envelope flap on which she (who knows when?) wrote in pencil

Spoken word is slave;
Unspoken is master.

Samuel Johnson wrote:

Every person is interesting if you tell his story right.

Honora is a strong and complex character.
But there's so much more to Edna's story that I will never know.

XXXV

Every time I shut off the TV I would then stand up, take a sharp left turn, and see the deer-mangled little dogwood tree through the glass-paned door. Its leaves fell and there it stood, surrounded by its bare-branched neighbors, encircled by its too-late plastic fence, covered on top by its too-late netting. "There you are," I told it. "If not for you on that hot, dry June 6, 2022, afternoon, my life would have taken a different turn."

A few people—not many—have asked how it would have been different.

I asked myself that.

I browsed through journals from the last few years and found, to my surprise, that I had been remembering a much more active person than I had been in years.

In those old journals, I found the me of two, three years ago asking whether I would "ever again have anything like my former energy." And then added, "But let's not overdo my memories of former energy." I often stayed in bed, drawing pictures or sometimes lying completely still for what seemed hours. I forgot to eat or skipped meals. I wondered how much longer my cat Zeb, now eighteen as I write this book, would live. I wondered how much longer I would live. On Sunday, November 8, 2020, I wrote, "I have thought considering my age & how I keep falling in the house—bruises everywhere— that I could experiment with writing my scenes faster. See what a faithful schedule could accomplish during the deep winter months."

As I approached the end of part 1 of my new novel, I wondered how I was going to flesh out the next part, which would follow two amazing months in which my five main people—father, three daughters, and the live-in governess who has arrived by helicopter on top of their remote bald mountain, will surpass themselves in learning from one another before the dark clouds gather. I wondered whether I should strike an ominous note to alert the careful reader, and gratify the rereader ("Aha! I spotted that!").

I consulted my old standby, *The Turn of the Screw*, to see how James had handled his warning for the careful reader from his narrating governess:

> This at all events was for the time: a time so full that as I recall the way it went it reminds me of all the art I now need to make it a little distinct. What I

look back at with amazement is the situation I accepted.

Was that all? I had remembered it as much more! I would have to flesh it out, the idyllic part, AND sneak in a negative note of my own invention.

Perhaps it could be as simple as having the eleven-year-old girl, the uncanny one, say at a peak moment (she has just successfully tutored the four others—father, governess, her two older sisters—on how her ant colony behaves when a "scout" discovers a morsel of food) something like, "What if this is the day we all look back on as the best day of our lives?"

The spring of 2023 began to show itself with the first tiny leaves. Jolanta looked out the windows of the glass-paned doors of the TV corner.

"That tree is dead," she said.

"Oh, no! Do you really think so?"

She opened the glass door and strode across the lawn and fingered the branches.

"Yes," she pronounced. "The little dogwood tree is dead."

It was toward the end of April. I decided to ask the gardeners to dig it up. This should take place, I decided, on the first of May.

"Mayday!" Robert's second opera, *Pantagleize*, was based on Michel de Ghelderode's play, in which the innocent Pantagleize decides to greet everyone with "What a lovely day!"—which, unknown to him, is the signal for a revolution to begin. That was just the sort of thing that Robert loved. He got the widow's permission and went to work. "A farce to make you sad."

XXXVI

May 24, 2023, 7:48 A.M.

Rusa just returned from her daily half hour on her indoor exercise bike. She has lost six pounds of the thirty she gained while caring for her previous patient, the woman who refused to eat the same meal twice.

When people—not many—ask me how the last year of my life would have been different had I not gone out the afternoon of June 6, 2022, to water the little dogwood tree, I say, "I truly don't know. But I know this: I would never have met Agnes, Mrs. B., my roommate at the rehabilitation center; I would never have met Rusa."

Carrie, my closest thing to a daughter, made many, many phone calls, and through the hospital, the Archcare nursing service, and Rusa's own agent, Nino (another Georgian!), found Rusa, a nurse with twenty-four years of service. She went to Carrie's house in New Jersey to be interviewed and then she came to me, first for one week, and then for as long as I needed her.

XXXVII

Robert had written music for Martha Graham, the choreographer, and created his opera *Pantagleize* several years before we met at Yaddo, in Saratoga Springs. I saw a performance of *Pantagleize* at Brooklyn College soon after we got together, and we stayed together for twenty-nine more years.

During those years I wrote seven librettos for his musical works: two operas, four chamber operas, and one piece for radio. The radio piece, which was also staged in New York, was for Robert J. Lurtsema, the host of the classical music show *Morning Pro Musica* on Boston's WGBH. It is called "Remembering Felix," for narrator, cello, and piano, and features a number of voices (old and young, Japanese- and English-speaking, all spoken by Lurtsema, remembering a musician named Felix, who has just died. Its opening line was "I felt a pang . . ."

Our first chamber opera, for three singers and a wood-wind quartet, was *The Last Lover*, the last lover of course being God.

In our early days Robert and I walked or hiked almost every day. I called him the Mountain Goat because he strode ahead, up the steepest inclines, while I puffed and lagged behind. On a hike up a mountain one afternoon, he complained bitterly because he had been commissioned to write a work for the music festival Caramoor, in Katonah, New York, and the material sent to him by poets and librettists was uninspired, overly wordy, unmusical pages.

I was displeased with a story I had written about a woman who made a list of her lovers (more than sixty) for a man who said her past didn't matter to his love. I had unsuccessfully merged this with the story of Saint Pelagia, in fourth-century Antioch, a sort of female Don Juan known as "vain and variable of courage, lewdness of mind and body, and splendidness of her attire." Her hagiography tells of her vehement conversion by a bishop, who castigates himself for not serving God with the splendor of this woman's raiment. She is so impressed by his devotion that she casts off "every shadow of her former self." She begins life as Brother Pelagius, a monk, until a young nun under his care becomes pregnant. A judge banishes Pelagius for life. As nuns are laying him out for burial, he is discovered to be a woman.

Robert was attracted by the saint's story and, as we had only three singers at our disposal, we decided that Pelagia, a mezzo, would play herself and "Brother Pelagius," and the soprano and baritone double their roles as Pelagia's maid and the nun who falls in love with Pelagius and the bishop and the devil (who has been one of Pelagia's many lovers).

The piece opens with Pelagia passing through the circle of woodwind musicians and singing, "This musician reminds me of a man in my past." She and the maid try to remember who the lover was:

"Attractus? Severinus? Braga, the Black? Finian the Younger, or his brother, the Older? Little Nonnatus or Blandinus, the Bore?" I still find myself humming the words: "Ah, so many, so many . . . and sometimes I wonder how many more?"

To me, libretto writing with Robert was a lark. I could write as many lines as I wanted and Robert would pick and choose.

The final work we wrote together was called *The Other Voice: A Portrait of Hilda of Whitby in Words and Music.* We had four singers: Hilda, the most influential abbess in Anglo-Saxon Christendom; the young Princess Elfleda, whom Hilda raises to succeed her as abbess; Rolf the Reeve, the oversociable pagan manager of the monastery; and his brother Caedmon the herdsman, who will sing only to animals and trees until Hilda (aided by Rolf) turns him into a musician and the first-known Anglo-Saxon poet. We thought it was our best yet and arranged to have it published by the music publisher Selah. It has a striking cover of the stained-glass window of St. Hilda in Christ Church Cathedral in Oxford.

At the end, when old Rolf, whom Hilda has taught to read, comes to pay a last visit to the dying abbess, his mournful refrain is, "I must not let it show on my face . . ."

The Other Voice was first performed at Holy Cross Church in Kingston, New York. Our priest Tom Miller, from St. Gregory's in Woodstock, sang the baritone part of Rolf the Reeve.

The work with its same cast had its second performance at St. Michael's Episcopal Church in New York. Robert was very sick by then, but he was, as he said, "still vertical."

After the dinner on the lower floor, we had to climb a steep flight of stairs to the sanctuary for the performance.

Robert stood at the bottom of the stairs.

"Is there an elevator?" he asked.

Robert was a large man. Two much-larger men materialized on either side of him, grasped him under the arms, and transported him to the top.

His feet never touched the ground.

XXXVIII

Mayday arrived. The gardeners came with shovels and rakes, took down the fencing around the tree and the netting on top, and dug up the little dogwood tree. They laid it to rest in the woods behind the house. Then they raked and smoothed the dark soil, sprinkled the grass seed, and watered everything well with the hose.

ACKNOWLEDGMENTS

Evie Preston for asking the question that became the title of this book.

Jane Toby for typing my handwritten notebooks.

Moses Cardona, my agent and First Reader.

Nancy Miller for her astute editing of our tenth book together.

Harriet LeFavour for merging the revisions into the final manuscript.

Greg Villepique, copy editor.

College. Copyright © 1951, 1955 by the President and Fellows of Harvard College. Copyright © renewed 1979, 1983 by the President and Fellows of Harvard College. Copyright © 1914, 1918, 1919, 1924, 1929, 1930, 1932, 1935, 1937, 1942 by Martha Dickinson Bianchi. Copyright © 1952, 1957, 1958, 1963, 1965 by Mary L. Hampson. Used by permission. All rights reserved.

Pages 99 and 100: "Aubade" from *The Complete Poems of Philip Larkin* by Philip Larkin, edited by Archie Burnett. Copyright © 2012 by The Estate of Philip Larkin. Reprinted by permission of Farrar, Straus and Giroux. All Rights Reserved.

Page 107 and 115: Godwin, Gail. *A Southern Family*. New York: William Morrow, 2001.

Page 123 and 124: Godwin, Gail. "Working on the Ending." *New York Times*, December 10, 2010.

Page 129–30: Edel, Leon, *Henry James: A Life*, reprinted by permission of HarperCollins Publishers, 1978.

Page 133: Godwin, Gail. "For Samuel Beckett: More." *James Joyce Quarterly* 8, no. 4 (1971): 332–35, http://www.jstor.org/stable/25486925.

Pages 137 and 138–39: Knowlson, James R. *Damned to Fame: The Life of Samuel Beckett*, New York: Bloomsbury Publishing, 1996.

Page 155: Considine, Austin. "How Brian Cox Felt about That Big Episode 3 Twist in *Succession*" from *The New York Times* © 2023. The New York Times Company. All rights reserved. Used under license.

Page 160: Godwin, Gail. *Flora: A Novel.* New York: Bloomsbury Publishing, 2013.

A NOTE ON THE AUTHOR

GAIL GODWIN is a three-time National Book Award finalist and the bestselling author of more than a dozen critically acclaimed books, including the novels *Grief Cottage*, *Flora*, *Father Melancholy's Daughter*, and *Evensong*, and *Publishing*, a memoir. She has received a Guggenheim Fellowship, National Endowment for the Arts grants for both fiction and libretto writing, and the Award in Literature from the American Academy of Arts and Letters. She lives in Woodstock, New York. www.gailgodwin.com